continuing professional development | in education

D1079204

CPD: Primary–Secondary Transition

An introduction to the issues

Brian Boyd

Series editor: Brian Boyd
Published in association with the
Times Educational Supplement Scotland

Hodder Gibson

A MEMBER OF THE HODDER HEADLINE GROUP

The Publishers would like to thank the following for permission to reproduce copyright material:

Acknowledgements
From *Winnie the Pooh* © A.A. Milne. Published by Egmont Books Limited, London and used with permission.

Every effort has been made to trace all copyright holders, but if any have been inadvertently overlooked the Publishers will be pleased to make the necessary arrangements at the first opportunity.

Although every effort has been made to ensure that website addresses are correct at time of going to press, Hodder Gibson cannot be held responsible for the content of any website mentioned in this book. It is sometimes possible to find a relocated web page by typing in the address of the home page for a website in the URL window of your browser.

Orders: please contact Bookpoint Ltd, 130 Milton Park, Abingdon, Oxon OX14 4SB. Telephone: (44) 01235 827720. Fax: (44) 01235 400454. Lines are open 9.00–6.00, Monday to Saturday, with a 24-hour message answering service. Visit our website at www.hoddereducation.co.uk. Hodder Gibson can be contacted direct on: Tel: 0141 848 1609; Fax: 0141 889 6315; email: hoddergibson@hodder.co.uk

© Brian Boyd 2005
First published in 2005 by
Hodder Gibson, a member of the Hodder Headline Group
2a Christie Street
Paisley PA1 1NB

Impression number   10 9 8 7 6 5 4 3 2 1
Year   2010 2009 2008 2007 2006 2005

Cover illustration by David Parkin.
Typeset by Transet Limited, Coventry, England.
Printed and bound in Great Britain by CPI Bath.

A catalogue record for this title is available from the British Library

ISBN-10: 0-340-88992-6
ISBN-13: 978-0-340-88992-3

About the Author

Professor Brian Boyd is Reader in Education at the University of Strathclyde. He has previously been a teacher of English, a head teacher and Chief Adviser in Strathclyde. He has published widely in the academic press and educational journals, and is a frequent contributor to conferences on a range of educational issues. He is co-founder of Tapestry, an educational organisation whose aim is to promote new thinking about learning and teaching. He used to play on the right wing for Port Glasgow Juniors.

Foreword

The *Times Educational Supplement Scotland* is delighted to be associated with the publication of this prestigious new series of books devoted to key areas in the field of continuing professional development.

Since the newspaper's birth in 1965, we have always attempted to inform, educate, and occasionally entertain the Scottish teaching profession, as well as to encourage dialogue between all educational sectors. In recent years, our commitment to the concept of encouraging educationists to constantly reflect – and act – upon best practice has been most tangibly evident in the provision of an annual CPD supplement. This offers full and detailed examination of developments in CPD from both Scottish and international contexts, and we attempt to share best practice in a manner that is both accessible and valuable.

This series of books is another testimony of our commitment to CPD. Drawing on the experience of foremost Scottish practitioners, each book attempts to offer academic rigour with a lightness of delivery that is too often found wanting in the weightier tomes that populate many educational libraries, and which are consequently left unread, except by those approaching examinations – or job interviews.

In short, we hope that these books will be welcomed in the groves of academe; but we also believe that they deserve to be read – and acted upon – by a much wider audience: those teachers across Scotland, nursery, primary and secondary, who deliver the curriculum on a daily basis to our young people.

Neil Munro
Editor, *Times Educational Supplement Scotland*

Contents

Introduction

Primary/Secondary transition: pantomime horse or seamless robe?

We almost called this book *The Pantomime Horse: an introduction to primary/secondary transition* (hence the cover image), because there are significant numbers of schools throughout the country where primary/secondary transition arrangements resemble the actions of such a horse rather too closely for comfort, with the back legs sometimes blissfully unaware of the actions being performed by the front ones. But it would have been unfair to include in such a generic title those areas where better practice is displayed, and where transition arrangements try to offer a seamless continuity in the educational experience of their pupils. So whilst the title is indisputably duller than the original suggestion, it reflects more accurately the book's contents. The cover image, however, offers a timely reminder of what can happen when primary/secondary transition isn't all that it should be...

Brian Boyd February 2005

1 Primary and secondary schools – chalk and cheese?

> The Mock Turtle went on.
> 'We had the best of educations – in fact we went to school every day –'
> 'I've been to a day-school too,' said Alice. 'You needn't be so proud as all that.'
> 'With extras?' asked the Mock Turtle, a little anxiously.
> 'Yes' said Alice, 'we learned French and music.'
> 'And washing?' said the Mock Turtle.
> 'Certainly not!' said Alice indignantly.
> 'Ah, then, yours wasn't really a good school,' said the Mock Turtle in a tone of great relief.
> *Alice Through the Looking Glass*, Lewis Carroll

Myth and reality

Myths abound about primary and secondary schools. It is said that primaries are child-centred while secondaries are subject-centred. It is alleged that primaries are caring while secondaries are academic. It is even claimed that it is in the secondary school that the real learning begins, and that the primary stage is in some way simply a preparation. Primary teachers are regarded as generalists, while their secondary counterparts are specialists (and, some would argue, superior). Finally, advocates of primary education would say that primary teachers are experts in learning while secondary teachers are experts in teaching.

Few if any of these claims can be substantiated. Indeed, published reports on schools by Her Majesty's Inspectorate of Education (HMI) would suggest the differences within the sectors are as great as those between them.

Real differences

However, there is no doubt that differences do exist between primary and secondary schools:

Structure

Structurally, the differences are profound. In the primary school, a class has one teacher all day, every day for a year, at least. There may be the occasional visiting specialist, or a member of the senior staff may take the class to free the teacher for some other work, or another teacher with a specialist skill, for example in music or art, might take the class for an hour or so. But, in general, it is one teacher who teaches the whole curriculum to the whole range of children in one class of around 30 pupils. The pupils move on from Primary 1 (P1) through to P7, as a class. The exception to this is in those schools that are too small to have one class at each stage (and some 50 per cent of Scottish primaries schools fall in to this category) and have 'composite' classes. These can span one, two or even three stages – and in the smallest schools can include P1 to P7. But the principle is the same; one teacher teaches the whole range of the curriculum to the whole range of pupils throughout the year.

In the secondary, teachers teach only one or maybe two subjects and therefore it takes between 12 and 15 teachers to teach the same range of the curriculum in Secondary 1 (S1) as it took one teacher to do in P7. In most secondary schools, pupils are organised into classes of *mixed ability* based on information supplied from the primary schools associated with the secondary, thus continuing the pattern in primary. However, in many secondary schools, the practice of *setting* by prior attainment is increasing, and pupils are put into classes with others judged to be of similar ability, in some cases as early as the beginning of S1 (most commonly in maths), and in other subjects (typically, English and modern languages) by the beginning of S2. This practice has been encouraged by HMI (1996) and has been re-iterated in ministerial announcements about standards in schools (2003).

Philosophy

Philosophically, primary and secondary schools differ too. The curriculum in the primary school is based on the concept of broad *areas*, while in secondaries, *subjects* and *modes* dominate.

The history of this divergence goes back to the *Primary Memorandum* (1966) and to the reports of the Munn and Dunning committees (1977). The primary school has always sought to make connections across the areas of knowledge and the notion of the 'integrated day' was symbolic of this philosophy, even if it did not happen in practice as much as its proponents would have wished (HMI 1981). Secondary schooling has resisted any attempt, nationally, to challenge the hegemony of the subject. The Munn report considered cross-curricular approaches in its review of the S3 and S4 curriculum, but in the end restricted any such innovation to three areas of the curriculum (social and vocational skills; contemporary social subjects; and general science) – and only for the 'less able' pupils. It is significant that all three have all but disappeared from many schools.

Status

Finally, there are differences in status, real and perceived. In the not too distant past, secondary teachers were paid more, both on starting teaching and at the top of the pay scale. To this day, headteachers of two schools of equal size in terms of pupil numbers, one primary and one secondary, will be paid different salaries (there are no prizes for guessing which headteacher is paid more!). Now, even with an all-graduate profession, and, indeed, with a primary B.Ed. degree which provides four years of specialist preparation, primary teachers, as generalists, still find it difficult to be treated as equals to their secondary counterparts. One manifestation of this is the difficulty of attracting men into primary teaching, the teaching of young children still being seen as 'women's work'. The reality, however, is that few secondary teachers would be confident that they have the skills to teach a P1, or even a P7, class.

When the 5–14 Development Programme was launched in 1987 by the then Minister for Education Michael Forsyth, it was an attempt to blur the edges of these differences by having the same curricular structure from P1 through to S2. Later in this book, this attempt will be assessed, albeit with the advantage of hindsight, but at this point it is sufficient to say that the myths have proved more enduring than any of the real differences described above.

The pantomime horse

The problem of primary–secondary transition is not a new one. In 1980, Her Majesty's Deputy Senior Chief Inspector of Schools, Andrew Chirnside, used the metaphor of the pantomime horse to describe the attempts by primary and secondary schools to achieve progression and continuity in pupils' learning. He argued that, like the pantomime horse, primary and secondary schools would like to be moving in the same direction, but that it was difficult to get their legs moving in the rhythm, and it was not helped by the fact it was dark inside the costume. Not only that, when they tried to communicate, the sounds were muffled and could be drowned out by 'noises off'. He stopped short of saying that their efforts were laughable; the issue was much too important. Chirnside argued that around P5 and P6 you had the 'onset of difficulty', followed by the 'onset of specialism' in P7. It was his contention that, if the S1 and S2 curriculum did not provide continuity and progression, there would be an 'onset of alienation' for many pupils.

The historical context of this focus on the problems of discontinuity between primary and secondary schooling is important. The Munn and Dunning committees, looking at curriculum and assessment in the middle years of secondary school had reported and sweeping changes were underway. The Warnock report (1978) into the education of pupils with special educational needs (a term coined by the report) had been published in England and Wales, and had been followed in 1978 by a highly influential report from HMI in Scotland entitled *The education of pupils with learning difficulties in Scottish schools*, and radical change was underway in what used to be called remedial education. HMI had also just reviewed the progress of P4 and P7 education since the *Primary Memorandum* (1981), and there were concerns about the slow pace of change, particularly in upper primary. Thus, in the view of Chirnside and influential inspectorate colleagues such as Bill Gatherer, P6 to S2 was the next natural arena for change.

But, the omens were not propitious. The Munn report had reinforced the subject dominance of the secondary curriculum. The Dunning report had placed the spotlight on the examination system, and wholescale change was taking place. Would anyone in the secondary sector be prepared for further change and would S1 and S2, far less P6 and P7 be the top of anyone's list of priorities in education? The answer that came in 1983 was the establishment of the Programme Directing Committee of the Consultative Council on the Curriculum to examine education of the 10–14 age group. Its report caught the Scottish educational community by surprise by radical recommendations.

The Death of the 10–14 report – did it jump or was it pushed?

The 10–14 report, as it came to be called, was published in 1986, almost immediately after the cessation of the most protracted and acrimonious period of industrial action in the history of Scottish education. Indeed, the timing could not have been worse since it coincided with the arrival in the Scottish office of Michael Forsyth, a standard bearer of the New Right, with a mission to raise standards in Scottish schools. With its principle of 'professional autonomy within guidelines', the report's authors took a consensual, liberal approach, putting teachers at the heart of curriculum development. The very style of the report with its discursive and philosophical exploration of the aims of education, its quasi-poetic language ('the classroom crackles with subliminal signals') and its length (some 210 pages including appendices), was not in keeping with what was to become a more centralist approach to educational policy-making.

Roger and Hartley (1990) have described the post-1987 era in education as a move from 'debate followed by consensus' to 'consultation followed by imposition'. When, at a national conference in 1986 to launch the 10–14 report, a senior civil servant publicly questioned its conclusions, the committee that produced it was taken by surprise. Later, when Michael Forsyth launched the consultation paper 'Curriculum and Assessment: a Policy for the 90s', senior members of HMI, hitherto closely involved in every curriculum development, were also taken aback.

The Minister ordered that the 10–14 Report be subjected to a costing exercise, the first time any major curricular report initiative had been so scrutinised. The committee welcomed this suggestion, somewhat naively believing it to be a genuine, and innovative move. However, in the event, it was little more than a delaying tactic and a thinly disguised ruse to enable HMI to reject the report's conclusions. The costing was £150m to £182m, depending on the model, over eleven years, or less than

1 per cent of educational spending nationally. Not only was the report never implemented, but the consensual approach to educational policy-making was to be under attack for the next decade (Boyd, 1992).

The 10–14 report had advocated a middle-school concept without the structural changes associated with a change in the system. While middle schools, most commonly for pupils of the P6 to S2 stages, were widespread in England and Wales, they existed for a relatively short time only in Grangemouth, in the east of Scotland. The proposal that there should be new qualification open to practising teachers (like the Infant Endorsement for primary staff) enabling them to work with P6, P7, S1 and S2, moving, where appropriate, between the sectors, was designed to create teams of teachers specialising in the 10–14 age group, thus providing continuity and coherence in learning and teaching. It is interesting to note that in 2003, the Faculty of Education of the University of Strathclyde began the preparation of a postgraduate module for teachers focusing on the 10–14 age group. Thus, as more and more people are beginning to question the very basis of the 5–14 programme, the ideas of its predecessor, the 10–14 report are being revisited.

Learning and teaching

In 1987, with the 10–14 report effectively abandoned, and 5–14 programme recently launched, HMI began to take a closer look at primary and secondary schools. In their influential reports, *Effective Secondary Schools* (1988) and *Effective Primary Schools* (1989) It became clear that on the issue of effective learning and teaching, the similarities were greater than the differences. HMI found that there was a huge overlap in the characteristics of effective learning in primary and secondary classrooms. Looked at from the perspective of the teacher or of the pupils, the same characteristics of effective learning and teaching crop up time after time.

Some conditions for effective learning

HM Inspectors report that pupils learn effectively when they:

1 are motivated.
2 know the purpose and relevance of their current work.
3 go about their tasks in an orderly fashion.

4 are confident in using available resources and know where to turn when they need help.
5 show consideration for one another and their teachers.
6 persevere in the face of challenges and demonstrate a commitment to the work in hand.

Effective Secondary Schools (1988, p. 5)

Effective practice

HM Inspectors find that effective learning takes place in classrooms where teachers:

1 establish and maintain a good classroom ethos in which pupils are motivated to learn.
2 plan, prepare and organise lessons well and ensure that pupils are clear about what they have to learn.
3 recognise the need for good classroom organisation including the organisation of resources.
4 set a good example, and foster good relationships with pupils.
5 have high but attainable expectations of pupils in respect of both academic performance and behaviour.
6 provide tasks which are well matched to the needs, aptitudes and prior knowledge of individual pupils.
7 understand the role of language in learning.
8 ensure that pupils acquire knowledge, understanding and skills, are encouraged to become independent and responsible, and are able to work purposefully on their own and with others.
9 check that learning has taken place by ensuring that assessment is an integral part of classroom work, and that it provides diagnostic information on pupils' progress and information which can be used to evaluate their teaching and to inform parents.
10 support classroom learning with work done at home where this is appropriate and in accordance with school policy.

Effective Primary Schools (1989, p. 2)

The gap between primary and secondary schools is, therefore, more about systems, structures and emphases, rather than the fundamentals. This should give us some hope that, with some imagination and creativity, the two sectors can be brought closer together so as to achieve the 5–14 aims of 'coherence, continuity and progression'. If there is so much that is similar in the fundamental area of learning and teaching, what is the problem?

Underachievement P6 to S2: what is the evidence?

In their 1996 report, *Achievement for All*, HMI suggested that there was evidence that pupils in S1 and S2 did not make the kind of progress in attainment that might be expected of them based on evidence from the primary school. They pointed to evidence from three sources, namely, their own inspections, the Assessment of Achievement Programme (AAP) and international comparative studies of achievement, particularly in mathematics. The reasons given for this so-called 'dip' in attainment included the number of teachers which pupils saw in a week in S1 and S2, a figure which could be as high as 16 or 17 in some schools. This, they argued, led to fragmentation and incoherence, and HMI suggested that by means of intelligent timetabling of classes, using devices such as rotation (e.g. where, instead of each class having one period per week of history, geography and modern studies, they should have three periods per week of each for one third of the year). In addition, HMI felt that too many pupils were not challenged because classes tended to be mixed-ability, and recommended setting by attainment, particularly, but not exclusively, in English and maths. Finally, they felt that some teaching methods did not ensure that pupils spent enough time on task, and advocated more 'direct teaching'.

In their follow-up report, *Achieving Success in S1 and S2* (1997), HMI continued to advocate timetabling solutions, shifted the methodological focus to 'direct *interactive* teaching' [my emphasis]; they also moved away slightly from advocating setting, instead laying out a set of principles which should inform any decisions about class organisation.

Achieving Success in S1 and S2

The organisation of pupils by class or within the class should:

1 create conditions which motivate all pupils to make sustained progress in learning within a common curriculum framework.
2 be flexible in responding to pupils' academic, personal and social development.
3 make it clear that the achievements and progress of each pupil are valued.
4 promote teaching which builds on the prior learning and achievements of pupils.
5 free teachers to spend most of their time on direct teaching and enable pupils to work effectively on challenging tasks.

6 be feasible and appropriate in terms of its expectations of teachers and pupils.

Achieving Success in S1 and S2 (1977, p. 39)

It also suggested that for any subject to have a right to be included in the overcrowded S1/S2 curriculum, it should:

1 build on prior learning at the primary stage.
2 lead to enduring and worthwhile outcomes which can be reported within the 5–14 framework of levels and targets.
3 deal with skills and knowledge which could not be taught successfully through another subject in the S1/S2 curriculum.
4 be allocated sufficient time for effective teaching to take place, normally a minimum of 160 minutes per week over a sustained period and a total of at least 100 hours (with the possible exception of personal and social education).
5 provide a sound basis for subsequent study in depth.
6 be supported by appropriate staff and resources.

(*ibid*, p. 15)

The issue of primary–secondary transition was also the subject of the report, *Improving Achievements in Scottish Schools: A report to the Secretary of State for Scotland* (1998), of the ministerial task group set up to look at Scottish schooling. It, too, recommended setting (p. 23), a reduction in the size of classes (p. 27) and more direct teaching (p. 26).

It is interesting to note that most of these conclusions, while consistent, are highly contentious. The literature review on setting and mixed ability, commissioned by HMI to inform *Achievement for All*, did not support its conclusions. *Setting and Streaming* (Harlen and Malcolm, 1997) published separately by the Scottish Council for Research in Education (SCRE), suggested that there was little evidence that either setting or mixed ability, by itself, would guarantee improved attainment. This report pointed out the risks associated with setting including lower expectations, self-fulfilling prophecy and gender/socio-economic status variables.

A key problem is that while there is widespread acceptance of the 'dip' phenomenon (in England and Wales it is referred to as 'the Year 7 dip'), there is very little hard evidence that it has any serious long-term effect on pupil achievement (Paterson, 2003). Perhaps, if the move from primary to secondary reflects a developmental stage in children, or even a rite of passage for them and their parents, then the nature of the two institutions makes it inevitable that there will be some temporary levelling-off in attainment. On the other hand, it could be argued that if learning from P6 to S2 were more continuous and progressive, if prior learning were built on and if pupils' potential was realised in S1 and S2, then levels of attainment in S4–S6, as measured by examinations, would be so much higher than at present.

A question of values?

There seems to be a general perception among the teaching profession as well as the population at large that secondary education is somehow of a higher status than primary. Theories abound as to why this should be so: the fact that the teaching in the primary population is largely female and that up until recently the pay was less; the fact that there are no exams at the primary stage (though for the last ten years or so there have been 5–14 National Tests); the fact that the secondary staff are specialists, though in primary too it is an all-graduate profession; and, perhaps, the fact that subject specialism happens in the secondary while in primary there is a smaller number of 'subject areas'.

But, if primary teachers feel that they are valued less highly than their secondary counterparts, paradoxically, the pupils feel that they are less valued when they reach secondary that they were while in the primary school. They often feel lost, that they are not treated as responsible citizens of the school and that some teachers do not even know their names. There is some truth in these perceptions. In the late 1960s, the Guidance system was introduced into secondary schools in acknowledgement of the danger that pupils could slip through the net and not be known as individuals in large secondary schools. Recent research (Boyd and Lawson, 2003) suggests that Guidance is valued by the pupils, but there is still a feeling among S1 pupils that they are not treated by the staff in general as 'real people'.

Furthermore, the evidence from research and from HMI is clear that 95 per cent of primary schools are either good or very good in terms of 'ethos, learning and teaching and links with the community'. The Improving School Effectiveness Project (2001) found that primary teachers' morale was higher than their secondary counterparts and that they were more likely to be positive about pupils' learning. Hamill and Boyd (2000; 2001; 2003) found that primary schools were more likely to be successful in their attempts to include pupils with special educational needs than were secondaries.

Looking back; looking forward

There is a growing realisation that primary–secondary transition is major issue facing Scottish education at the beginning of the twenty-first century. Scotland's First Minister has called for new thinking in this area and there have been calls for a re-consideration of the 10–14 report (Times Educational Supplement Scotland, 14 March 2003). Perhaps a good starting point would be the curriculum.

The 5–14 curriculum, launched in 1987 in a consultation paper by the then Education Minister, Michael Forsyth, has been called into question in recent months by educationists. It has not lived up to the expectations of raising achievement and eliminating the 'fresh start' approach in S1. The transition from P7 to S1 is not the seamless garment we were promised, and despite some good initiatives in some schools, with 'bridging projects' and reciprocal visits, there is still evidence (Boyd and Simpson, 2000) of underachievement in S1 and S2. The complexity of the secondary timetable, the difficulty of sharing meaningful information about pupils' learning between the two sectors and the pressure in the secondaries of external examinations, all combine to ensure that the first two years of secondary education are not, apparently, a priority for anyone – except, perhaps, the pupils themselves.

If, indeed, schooldays are the best days of our lives, then it would appear that S1 and S2 represent a hiatus, a blip on the screen, a photograph in the album which is out of focus. It is unclear just what the aims of education are in S1 and S2. It used to be that they provided a common course, a settling in period, an opportunity to assess pupils before the 'real work' of exams kicked in. Now with 5–14, S1 and S2 should represent a seamless link with the learning that has taken place in the primary school. However, there is evidence that the 'fresh start' approach is alive and well – and flourishing. How then, do we bridge the gap?

P6 to S2: something's got to give

It is difficult to see how the present approach to P6 to S2 can continue, given the mounting concerns about underachievement.

However, as councils across Scotland rebuild their ageing schools, funding them through the Public Private Partnership (PPP) approach, they are continuing to build secondary schools and primary schools, enshrining the traditional structures within new, high-tech buildings. There are other pressures in the system which may force change to take place in an *ad hoc* way. The McCrone agreement, *A Teaching Profession for the 21st Century*, has for the first time given primary teachers an entitlement of two and a half hours per week non-class contact time within the pupil day. This means that class teachers will need to be relieved of their classroom duties for that period of time each week, and already some council education departments are looking at engaging more 'specialists' for this purpose.

Thus the idea, often expressed in the past, but never implemented, that there should be more specialism in the upper primary and more generalism in the lower secondary, may be about to be implemented for pragmatic reasons. In the secondary sector, traditional subject departments are being collapsed or amalgamated, at least for management purposes, and it may be that as Initial Teacher Education (ITE) faculties increase their demands for entrants into secondary courses to have two or even three teaching subjects, teams of teachers may emerge, working inter-departmentally and maybe even cross-sectorally to try to provide continuity, progression and coherence in the curriculum, P6 to S2.

The question is, will these *ad hoc* responses to pressures in the system lead to reasoned and well-considered improvements in primary–secondary transition?

SUMMARY

While some of the differences between primary and secondary schools are superficial, there are key distinctions which can be drawn in terms of structure, philosophy and status. Nevertheless, successive HMI reports in the 1980s suggested that the principles of effective learning and teaching in each sector were the same. Attempts to look at the issue of transition in the 1980s, notably *Education 10–14 in Scotland* fell foul of the New Right ideology personified by Michael Forsyth in the Scottish Office. In the 1990s, HMI focused their attention on S1 and S2, recommending, among other things, more *setting* by attainment and *direct interactive teaching*. Recent studies in Scotland have suggested that the 5–14 programme has not solved the problems of transition and have confirmed that the fresh start approach in S1 is alive and well. However, now, in the post-McCrone era, there are signs that some of the 'generalist' versus 'specialist' barriers may be being broken down and some local authorities are moving towards 10–14 style solutions. ITE is also beginning to look seriously at the concept of the generic teacher who can move between primary and secondary.

POINTS FOR REFLECTION

1. Are the differences between primary and secondary necessary and a reflection of the different needs of young people, or are they simply the result of a number of historical decisions which are no longer valid or helpful?

2. Would Chirnside's metaphor be too harsh a criticism of what is happening now in Scottish schools? Has, for example, the emergence of clusters of schools or Learning Communities or Families of Schools, begun to improve the situation?

3. Is the 10–14 report worth revisiting? Is 5–14 nearing the end of its 'shelf-life'? Is the middle school concept likely to find any favour in the twenty-first century?

2 Moving on

> 'And how many hours a day did you do lessons?' asked Alice.
> 'Ten hours the first day,' said the Mock Turtle, 'nine hours the next, and so on.'
> 'What a curious plan!' exclaimed Alice.
> 'That's the reason they're called lessons,' the Gryphon remarked, 'because they lessen from day to day!'
> *Alice Throught the Looking Glass*, **Lewis Carroll**

Settling in

Is the curriculum part of the problem or part of the solution? For a long time it was assumed that the different curriculum structures of primary and secondary schools were at the root of the problem of the discontinuity experienced by pupils moving from P7 to S1. However, since the launch of the 5–14 programme in 1987, it could be argued that the curriculum ought not to be problematic. All of the Guidelines documents on the areas of the curriculum identified by the 5–14 programme apply equally to S1 and S2 and P1 to P7. The five key principles of the programme, *breadth*, *balance*, *continuity*, *coherence* and *progression* also apply to both sectors, as do the structure of the various areas of the curriculum, including *strands*, *programmes of work* and *levels* of attainment, A to F. And, of course, national tests are administered, as appropriate, in both primary and secondary school.

However, this apparent 'seamless robe' of curricular structure belies the reality of the differences between the sectors. Indeed, to paraphrase the old adage about Britain and the United States, primaries and secondaries are two sectors separated by a common curriculum. Just when we thought a common terminology to describe the curriculum would obviate the difficulties experienced in the past when primary and secondary teachers gathered together, it would appear that 5–14 has done little more than paper over the cracks.

The evidence from research (Boyd and Simpson, 2000) suggests that pastoral care at the point of transfer from primary to secondary school is generally very good. Particularly in the case of vulnerable pupils, staff from the secondary school – support for learning, Guidance, subject specialists and senior managers – work alongside their primary colleagues to ensure that transition is smooth. Throughout the pupils' P7 year, there are visits to the secondary school as well as visits to the primary from former pupils and from secondary teachers. For parents there are often open evenings in the secondary school as well as evening consultation meetings in each of the associated primary schools. There may be shared sports days, competitions involving primary and secondary pupils working together in teams, and exchanges of work from former P7 pupils now at secondary to their P7 counterparts. And there will be publications aimed at pupils and their parents in preparation for the transition. Much of this is above and beyond the call of duty for staff in both sectors, and research suggests that pupils and parents appreciate these efforts.

In 2000, Highland Health Board, in association with the Highland Council and The Health Education Board for Scotland, published a report entitled *Moving On: the emotional well-being of young people in transition from primary to secondary school*. The impetus for the research project which led to the publication was the belief that many young people experienced anxiety when transferring from primary to secondary school. A whole cohort of P7 pupils across Highland region was targeted with a view to 'mapping their experiences' (p. 2) and a number of primary and secondary schools were selected as case studies. The researchers found that two-thirds of pupils have some anxieties about the transition from primary to secondary school, though only one in ten pupils reported that they were 'genuinely worried' about it (p. 3). One of the key reasons for the relatively low levels of anxiety was felt to be 'the effective procedures for ensuring a smooth transition form primary to secondary schooling' instigated by the schools (p. 3). Many of the schools had policies in place regarding transition, most had a member of staff designated to manage the transition and all of the clusters of schools had a wide range of activities and events throughout the year as part of their primary-secondary liaison programme.

The report collated the 'factors critical to an effective transition' (p. 6) as indicated by school staff in primaries and secondaries; see the table below:

Ranking	Factors critical to an effective transition
1st	Effective primary-secondary liaison with good two-way communication between the same contacts and information on pupils which goes beyond academic attainment
2nd	Opportunities for P7s to become familiar with secondary staff and the secondary school before transfer
3rd	Induction visits which provide opportunities for P7s to work on an S1 curriculum timetable and in the classes to which they will be allocated
4th	Ensure that there are identified persons to whom the S1 can turn for help who will provide a consistent and effective response
5th	Continuity of curriculum from P7 to S1
6th	Opportunities for P7s to get to know P7s in other primary schools before transfer
7th	Visits to primaries by subject specialists as well as guidance and learning support staff

The report also reported that parents were, in the main, satisfied with the arrangements for transfer. It recommended that all schools learn from the best practice of others and suggested, *inter alia*, that the visit to the secondary in the summer term of P7 should be a week in duration and for there to be proactive programmes designed to give pupils 'coping skills' so that they might make the most of their early days and weeks in the secondary school.

It's the curriculum, stupid

Perhaps the most surprising finding from the *Moving on* study was that 'continuity of the curriculum' came in at a lowly 5th place in the ranking of 'factors critical to an effective transition'.

Among the possible reasons for this are the fact that staff do not expect there to be much continuity or even that they do not feel that pupils expect it either. Perhaps there is still a belief in the 'fresh start' approach in S1, a sense that change is the name of the game and curricular continuity is neither possible nor desirable.

In fact, while there are no villains in this piece of the Scottish education system, there are some illogicalities which almost defy explanation and which have become the stuff of myth and folklore. Let's look at some of the strange phenomena surrounding P7 to S1 curriculum structures:

Strange phenomenon number 1

Why do most secondary schools have a 30-period week and, therefore, a 6-period day? Why does this configuration result in periods which vary from 54 to 60 minutes (not counting Registration periods of 10 minutes or so)? Why, in some schools, do periods begin at, say, 10.01 and finish at 10.57? And why, if one period ends at 11.52, does the next one begin at 11.53, thus ensuring that pupils will necessarily be late for their next class if they have to walk the entire length of the school from one department to the other?

Strange phenomenon number 2

Why do primary schools have their English language and mathematics only in the mornings? Is there research evidence that humans learn most effectively before noon? Are maths and English unique in the demands they place on children's concentration? Are science, history, technology, and the arts best done in the afternoon because… (readers may add their own answer!)

Strange phenomenon number 3

Why does it take up to fifteen teachers to teach the same curriculum in S1 which one teacher managed in P7? Does environmental studies alone need to be taught by around six or seven secondary teachers? And is this the reason why continuity and progression are so difficult to achieve? If secondary and primary teachers rarely have the chance to talk to one another about learning and teaching or about pupils' progress, is it surprising that the 'fresh start' approach in S1 is alive and well?

There is nothing which cannot be changed in education, nothing which cannot be achieved in the school timetable. It is all a matter of priorities. Not everything can be done at once, and every action has a consequence. Boyd and Simpson (2000) found that few secondary teachers saw S1 as their top priority, while P7 is a very important stage in the primary school. Perhaps we need to get back to first principles?

From principles to practice

The five principles of the 5–14 programme are worth looking at in some detail insofar as they apply to the curriculum.

1 Continuity

Continuity ensures that learning builds on pupils' previous experience and attainment.

(*The structure and balance of the curriculum 5–14* p. 6)

The difficulties of continuity are often seen as being *practical*. It has always assumed that since pupils in the primary have only one teacher for most of the subject areas while in the secondary school a first-year pupil might meet fifteen different teachers in a week, then the curriculum *has* to be different. Not only that, the secondaries had to organise themselves into roughly hour-long *periods*, while the primaries had the whole day (it used to be called the 'integrated day') in which pupils could move seamlessly from one topic to another. However, the question which has to be asked is whether secondary schools *have* to organise themselves in this way, or do they simply choose to do so, for reasons associated with the demands of external examinations? Ironically, as a consequence of the 5–14 curriculum, primary schools have long since abandoned what used to be seen as a 'seamless robe' of learning, in favour of a more timetabled approach. Thus, 5–14 has brought the practicalities of organising learning and teaching into periods of time in the primary and in the secondary closer together without necessarily making content or methodology more continuous.

As indicated in Chapter 1, the differences may also be *philosophical*. Since the secondary curriculum has it origins in the kind philosophy espoused by Paul Hirst (1976) which sees 'forms of knowledge' as being 'logically prior to the characteristics of the child', then it is easy to see why the subject reigns supreme in the secondary school. The Munn Report

(1977) on the curriculum in S3 and S4 of secondary schools considered the advantages and disadvantages of a cross-curricular approach, and rejected it for all but the less academic pupils. This further cemented the place of the subject in S1 and S2, often seen by secondary teachers as little more than a preparation for S3 and S4 (Boyd and Simpson, 2000). Thus, when the 5–14 programme replaced the 10–14 proposals, it failed to address the fundamental difference between the way in which the two sectors viewed the structure of the curriculum. To assume that by applying the same set of Guidelines to P1–P7 and to S1 and S2 that if would somehow be 'all right on the night' was either naïve or disingenuous. In the event, it became clear that the seven or so secondary subjects which were encompassed by the single curricular area environmental studies had little likelihood of ever working together in harmony. Indeed, even where there was a one-to-one correspondence between the sectors, as in English language or mathematics, curricular continuity has been problematic in parts of the country, partly because of lack of time for teachers to meet together, and partly because of differences in perspective between the sectors as to how the subject should be taught.

2 Progression

> **Progression** provides pupils with a series of challenging but attainable goals.
>
> (*ibid*, p. 6)

The lack of progression in pupils' learning between P7 and S1 may be seen as a problem of *communication*. If there is a lack of satisfactory progression in the child's learning, it may be because either the secondary staff do not have what they perceive to be adequate information from the primary schools, or they still believe in the 'fresh start' approach dismissed by HMI in the 1993 report. In their study of the first two years of secondary schooling in a council in Scotland, Boyd and Simpson (2000) uncovered some unreconstructed views among *some* secondary staff.

> I don't really mind what information comes from the primary school. I start teaching them History when they get here.
>
> (Principal teacher of History)

> You can't trust the assessments from the primary school. They're all over the place.
>
> (Principal Teacher of Maths)

Perhaps the best example of all was when the depute headteacher of a secondary school stood up in front of the staff on the first in-service day of the year and held up a folder. She informed the staff that this was a P7 'Best Work' folder and that she now had all of them for the in-coming S1 pupils (who would be arriving the next day). She had arranged them in boxes for each of the new S1 classes and asked the heads of department to let her know when they would like to collect them so that they could be looked at during a departmental meeting. Later, when asked how many departments had asked for the folders, she agreed that she had 'not been knocked down in the rush'. In fact, only three had done so.

The problem was not that the secondary teachers were lazy or recalcitrant; it was simply that they felt that the folders contained the wrong kind of information for them as subject specialists. Despite the fact that the primary teachers had spent many hours with their pupils ensuring that the folders were indeed their best work, the secondary staff saw little value in the product!

Progression is something which many feel should happen automatically, with age and maturation. Jean Piaget's work on child development was very influential in the philosophy of the government report, *The Primary Memorandum* of 1965. He introduced the idea of 'stages' of development and set in motion in Scotland the whole idea of child-centred learning. But were his ideas misunderstood? Were they too theoretical for the average primary teacher to accommodate in the classroom? Farqhuarson (1990) has argued that they were, and that there was too big a gap between the policy-makers and the policy-implementers so that when HMI looked at P4 and P7 in their 1981 report, they seemed genuinely disappointed in the relative lack of progress in the policy's implementation. But what if Piaget's theory had, in a real sense, been misinterpreted? What if children do not progress in clear-cut, predictable stages; if, as Lipman has argued, they are capable of conceptual thinking as early as P1 and P2; and if, as Vygotsky has suggested, learning is a social process and children are able to construct meanings in collaboration with others, is there not a chance that pupils in S1 are hindered in their learning because of lowered expectations of what they can achieve? Progression may not be something that simply happens or does not happen; it may be that teachers in primary schools and in secondary schools have to share, in a more sustained and face-to-face way than at present, their insights into how pupils actually learn.

3 Coherence

Coherence requires the establishment of links across the various areas of learning so that pupils begin to make connections between one area of knowledge and skills and another.

(*ibid* p. 6)

Coherence has often been seen as the preserve of the primary school. Having one teacher who teachers everything is surely the best way of ensuring coherence. Or is it? Some have argued that the onset of the 5–14 curriculum and the demise of the topic approach, pioneered so effectively by Bill Michael, Fred Rendall, Steve Bell and their colleagues in the Primary Education department of Jordanhill College in the 1960s (Harrison and Marker, 1996) was the death-knell of coherence. Alan Macdonald has written eloquently and passionately about the effect that 5–14 had on the primary curriculum in 'Themes and Subjects' (in Kirk and Glaister, 1994) and reserves his most trenchant criticism for the 'poisoned pie' of environmental studies. Thus, if coherence has become more difficult in the primary school, with its timetabled day of English language followed by maths followed by environmental studies or expressive arts or religious and moral education or even modern languages, what of the S1 and S2 curriculum? Surely, amidst all the concerns about primary–secondary transition, from the 10–14 report onwards, there must be less fragmentation in S1 and S2?

Not necessarily! Even with HMI advocating timetabling devices such as rotation, and with teacher education institutions trying to attract teachers qualified in two or even three subjects, few schools if any have reduced the number of teachers which an S1 pupil meets in a week to below twelve. One or two have reached ten, but only by arbitrarily removing some subjects from S1 and beginning them in S2. A few schools offer limited choice of subjects at the end of S1, thus reducing the overall number which a pupil studies; however, the S1 and S2 curriculum in many schools has changed little in the last twenty years.

In the secondary school, this problem is compounded by the lack of opportunity for staff to discuss learning and teaching with colleagues in other departments. A device used by the present writer when doing in-service work with secondary schools illustrates the point. When a whole secondary school staff are assembled, they are asked to think of a colleague of the same age or length of experience in teaching who does not work in their department, preferably who teaches a subject not linked in any way to theirs. They are asked to look at the person, briefly, but not to stare, since that is rude! They are then asked the simple question, 'When was the last time you saw this colleague teach?' The answer, in 95 per cent of cases is 'Never'. So, there we have it. Upwards of 60 teachers, trained in a similar way, working in the same school, teaching the same children in many cases, but who never have the opportunity to see one another teach. Not only that, but ordinarily they may not have much opportunity to talk to one another at any length about learning and teaching generally, or about specific classes or pupils whom they share.

Coherence, to put it bluntly, is for many teachers a luxury which they cannot afford. For pupils, it might make the difference between 'deep' and 'surface' learning (Entwistle, 1981). If making connections is at the heart of learning, the present curriculum structures do not seem to be making a positive contribution.

4 Breadth

> Breadth provides appropriate experiences to ensure the coverage of a sufficiently comprehensive range of areas of learning.
>
> (*ibid*, p. 6)

Scotland has long been proud of the breadth of its curriculum, in the primary school, in the secondary and especially at the level of Highers in S5. Traditionally, Scottish pupils have taken up to five Highers, unlike their counterparts in England and Wales who normally take no more than three A2 levels in upper sixth. Some commentators (Paterson 2003) have pointed out that breadth may well, in fact, be one of the enduring myths of Scottish education, more an aspiration than a reality. If a student takes five Highers in English, maths, physics, chemistry and geography, or English, French, Spanish, history and modern studies, how much breadth is there in reality?

However, there is mandatory breadth in the middle years of the Scottish secondary school with all pupils required to study each of eight 'modes' (see below), the only choice being among subject within modes. Since the present structure was introduced in 1977 (Munn and Dunning reports) there has been ongoing debate about whether breadth should mean that all pupils must do the same subjects. Can one person's breadth be another's restricted choice? Does the school take into account learning which takes place in the community or in other establishments and should, for example, a gifted musician, playing in a band or orchestra and taking examinations with one of the established boards, still have to fulfil the creative and aesthetic mode? Some subjects, such as modern languages, have had to fight for a place in the compulsory core of subjects which all pupils must take, and yet, paradoxically, they have come under pressure from pupils and others to be made optional.

However, the foundation of this breadth at upper secondary is the 5–14 curriculum, and *The Structure and Balance of the Curriculum 5–14* sets it out in tabular form on p. 12 to reflect the different structures and terminology of the primary and secondary schools:

Curricular Area	5–14 Guidelines	Mode
Language	English language Gaelic Latin Modern languages	Language and communication
Mathematics	Mathematics	Mathematical activities and applications
Expressive arts	Expressive arts	Creative and aesthetic activities Physical education
Environmental studies	Environmental studies	Scientific studies and applications Social and environmental studies Technological activities and applications
Religious and moral education	Religious and moral education Personal and social development	Religious and moral education

The immediate problem is graphically illustrated and that is the move from five curricular areas in P7 to eight modes in the secondary. It is, however, even more problematic than it at first seems because the eight modes only apply from S3 onwards. In fact, the move, as has already been indicated, is from five curricular areas to upwards of fourteen different subjects! Thus while breadth is present in both primary and secondary school, it is, in reality, a different kind of breadth.

The question must also be posed as to whether breadth is always, in itself, a good thing. 'Specialism' and 'generalism' have been, throughout the centuries, been valued differently by societies. The concept of 'Renaissance Man' was of the generalist, the person who could aspire to know everything there is to know. Leonardo da Vinci may be the most famous of such individuals, but as scientific knowledge grew, so too did specialisms, and in our present age, it is these which are most highly regarded. Thus the concept of the absent-minded professor, brilliant in his own field, but blissfully unaware of what is happening in the world around him, in popular culture and, indeed, in terms of interpersonal relationships, has entered the folklore. In education, primary teachers are generalists while secondary teachers are specialists, and there can be a resultant gap in the value attributed to each. For the pupils, the Scottish education system still promotes a message of breadth, but there are those who see it as the enemy of 'depth', and they worry that the pupils skim over the surface of too many curricular areas and study none of them in depth.

5 Balance

> **Balance** ensures that appropriate time is allocated to each area of curricular activity and that provision is made for a variety of learning experiences.
>
> *(ibid,* p. 6)

Figure 1 in *The Structure and Balance of the Curriculum 5–14 (1993)* represents 'the balance of allocation of time' by a set of concentric circles. The five curricular areas and the eight modes (above) are given a slice of the weekly cake, expressed as a percentage. Thus, in the primary, the following is given as the minimum allocations of time to be apportioned to each area:

Language	15%
Mathematics	15%
Environmental studies	25%
Expressive Arts	15%
Religious and Moral education	10%

In the secondary, the allocation to the modes is as follows:

Language and Communication	20%
Mathematical studies and applications	10%
Scientific studies and applications	10%
Social and environmental studies	10%
Technological activities and applications	10%
Creative and aesthetic activities	10%
Physical education	5%
Religious and moral education	5%

In each case, the astute reader will have noticed that the total is only 80 per cent, since 'an allocation of 20 per cent of time is made in both primary and secondary to allow for flexibility.' (p. 16).

Expressed like this, it is difficult to know how the allocations were arrived at or how they were to be applied. For example, is the same balance appropriate in P1 as it is in P7? How flexible is the flexibility factor? The report suggested that it could be used for:

> ...dealing with cross-curricular issues; for learning support and enrichment; for pastoral care; for whole-school activities; or for opportunities for learning which may arise from contemporary events or issues.
>
> (*ibid*, p. 17)

The reality in many schools, however, suggests that there is *de facto* little flexibility left when demands are placed on school such as early intervention initiatives, primary modern foreign languages, new reading schemes, circle time, anti-bullying initiatives, target-setting, and most recently, Assessment is for Learning. A recent PhD thesis (Gallastegi, 2004) found that the vast majority of schools fail to allocate the modern foreign language its recommended 90 minutes per week. Most primary teaches when asked why they find it difficult to introduce new ideas such as thinking skills, cite the pressure of the curriculum as the main obstacle. Thus, whether as a fact or a perception, the balance of the curriculum as expressed in percentages of the weekly time available, often puts pressure on teachers to 'get through the curriculum'. Simpson has described this phenomenon as 'coverage' (Boyd and Simpson, 2000), and it applies as much to secondary staff as it does to primary.

In 2001, the Scottish Executive Education Department (SEED) issued a circular to all local authority schools encouraging them to introduce more flexibility. HMCI Philip Banks, speaking at a conference in Glasgow in 2002, re-iterated this encouragement to schools to show 'creativity, innovation and flexibility' and to feel free to depart from national guidance provided three criteria are met:

- The change must have as its goal the improvement of learning and teaching.
- It must have been the subject of widespread consultation with all stakeholders.
- It must be monitored and evaluated.

In England and Wales, the rigidity caused by too centralised a prescription of the primary curriculum is implicitly acknowledged by the fact that the report *Excellence and Enjoyment* (DfES 2003) lists the 'existing and planned freedoms' which the Government is prepared to give to teachers including:

- how to teach,
- which aspects of subject pupils will study in depth,
- how long to spend on each subject,
- how to arrange learning in the school day, and
- to use sections of previous or later programmes of study. (p. 17)

Primary teachers might be forgiven for saying that these are the freedoms they should enjoy if they are trusted to be reflective professionals!

An example encapsulates the challenge facing schools. The Government's early intervention schemes, designed to raise attainment among pupils experiencing social disadvantage, was widely welcomed by everyone concerned. Now, some four years after the first scheme was introduced, some evidence is emerging (Leslie, 2003) that while all pupils in the early years of primary seem to be benefiting from some early intervention schemes, it is the most advantaged children who are benefiting most. Thus the gap which early intervention was set up to narrow, is actually widening. One challenge is, how flexible will schools be allowed to be in changing the balance of the curriculum in order to try to redress this imbalance? The curriculum has been described as a selection from the culture of a society. What is certainly true is that it is neither fixed nor immutable. It changes from generation to generation, reflecting new theories, new demands, new fashions and new political imperatives. Perhaps it is time to ask if the present curriculum structure is meeting the needs of pupils as they move from primary to secondary school.

Middle schools – a structural solution?

Scotland has never embraced the middle school concept, with the exception of the Grangemouth experiment. However, to this day, parts of the UK continue to organise their schooling on the lines of junior schools, middle schools and high schools. Such a system has obvious advantages. It acknowledges that transition from one kind of school to another is important as children mature, but tries to smooth the process by making it less abrupt and more continuous. The pupils attend the junior school until (in Scottish terms) the end of P5. They then move to the middle school and begin P6. Since the structure of the curriculum, the learning and teaching approaches and the class organisation are similar to what they have experienced in the junior school, the pupils tend to find the transition to middle school relatively straightforward. The evidence suggests that there is less underachievement associated with transition at this stage, and the coming together of pupils from a number of junior schools, the formation of new classes and the encounter with new teachers appears to happen with minimal traumatic effect.

In the middle school, P6 and P7 may be organised on very similar lines to the conventional primary school. However, the existence within the school of staff who have been trained as secondary specialists, and whose main focus is S1 and S2, enables the school to blur the edges to the traditional primary and secondary school. Teachers may find themselves operating across P6 to S2 and, in the English system, working across a range of subjects. The move from P7 to S1 happens within the same building and with many of the same staff involved. The S1 and S2 pupils are the oldest in the middle school and assume responsibilities which they would rarely be accorded in the secondary school.

The problem arises when pupils make the move to the high school at the end of S2. In England at present, this move takes place in the middle of Key Stage Three, an important point within the National Curriculum at the end of which schools are measured in terms of pupil performance in SATS. Thus, not only are all the normal issues associated with transition from primary to secondary present, but they are exacerbated by the imminence of this national judgement of pupil – and school – performance. However, in the Scottish system, this transition would take place at the beginning of the Standard Grade phase of schooling where there are no SATS. Indeed, in the present 5–14 system, where secondary schools feel under pressure to achieve certain targets in terms of numbers of pupils achieving Level F, this 'pressure', real or perceived, would be a feature of the middle school. middle schools might also be in a better position to address the phenomenon of the S2 (Year 8) dip in achievement. S2, in the Middle school, would be a significant stage, the pupils' final year, and pinnacle rather than a dip, and S3, already a transition point from 5–14 to Standard Grade, would be a more natural break point in the process of schooling.

What is the evidence from England?

In 1996, Suffolk Education department carried out an investigation into what happens when pupils transfer into their next schools at the age of 9, 11 and 13. Data was collected as part of the Suffolk School Improvement Project which seemed to show that there was a dip in progress in reading when pupils transfer from one phase of schooling to another. Across the Local Education Authority (LEA), they found that:

> Pupils who are in 5–11 schools make more progress on average between the ages of nine and eleven than do pupils who transfer to middle schools. Similarly pupils in middle schools make more progress in reading in Key Stage 3 than do pupils who transfer at eleven into high schools. Inspection evidence also suggests that the quality of work in year 9 in upper schools is weaker than elsewhere in those schools.   (p. 3)

The LEA then undertook a 'transfer investigation' involving 360 pupils who were observed in the months before transfer and in the months after. Named pupils in Years 4, 6 and 8 were observed in their classrooms before transfer and then again when they had moved to their new schools and were in Years 5, 7 and 9. The conclusions from this study were interesting and in some respects similar to research in Scotland.

Schools are good at preparing pupils for their new schools and making sure that they settle into new routines.
This is in line with the Boyd/Simpson report (2002) which found that staff from secondary support for learning, Guidance and subject departments liaised well with primary staff to smooth the transfer of pupils. Parents' meetings were held, visits of pupils organised and documentation produced – all designed to ensure that pupils transferred as smoothly as possible.

Building on the prior attainment of pupils when they transfer is a major weakness of the system.
The situation varied across first to middle, primary to high school and middle to upper. Overall, upper schools tended to be better at building on pupils' prior attainment but the report commented that 'there is no cause for complacency'. The situation was worst in mathematics and reading.

In general, expectations of incoming pupils are too low.
The report used the same phrase as the Boyd/Simpson report and suggested that 'the 'fresh start' approach is detrimental to pupils' progress.

Transfer documentation on pupil attainment is not used effectively by the receiving schools.
Even within the structure of the National Curriculum, schools did not make good use of the information received. Often test scores were used to group or set pupils and some schools even set their own tests on entry. While practice for pupils with additional support needs was exemplary, for the others the information often did not reach the teachers who needed to see it.

Cross-phase (cross-sectoral) meetings of teachers varied in frequency and in usefulness.
These meetings tended to work best when pupils' work was the main focus. Where there had been time freed up to enable teaches to teach in one another's schools, the benefits were huge.

Suffolk Education Department 1996

It would appear that transfer from one school to another, irrespective of the age and stage when it happens, is problematic. The issues may be slightly different from one subject area to another and from one stage to another, but there is a common thread running through these studies of poor information transfer, a 'fresh start' approach and failure to build on prior learning. The final sentence in the Suffolk report sums up the frustrations of those trying to improve matters:

> It is very largely for the receiving school to do something about it.

However, it is what to do, given the constraints of the curriculum, of time and of staff priorities, that remains the key question.

SUMMARY

In general, arrangements for the transition from primary to secondary school in Scotland are good. Research has shown that schools go to considerable lengths to smooth the transition of all pupils, particularly those who are vulnerable. However, curricular discontinuity remains a formidable problem. The five curricular principles of the 5–14 programme – breadth, balance, continuity, coherence and progression – have all proved to be problematic and where they have in fact been implemented, it is often in a mechanistic and prescriptive manner. Middle schools have only been tried once in Scotland, and rejected. The 10–14 Report recommended a 'middle school concept' without the buildings, but was also rejected, and evidence from England suggests that middle schools do not solve all of the problems of discontinuity.

POINTS FOR REFLECTION

1 From your own experience, what are the pluses and minuses of the current approach to primary–secondary transition?

2 Are the present principles of breadth, balance, continuity, coherence and progression:
   i) the only principles which should inform the curriculum?
   ii) being achieved in our schools at present?

3 Is the curriculum still the problem?

4 Three 'strange phenomena' are highlighted in this chapter. Can you add to this list?

3 Teachers – help or hindrance?

> In the classroom, loving the children to understanding.
>
> **Maya Angelou**

Primary and secondary – ne'er the twain shall meet?

In Scotland, as in the rest of the British Isles, initial teacher education (ITE), or teacher training, as it used to be called, is done by sector. In other words, since 1983, there have been three main routes to becoming a teacher:

- Four-year BEd (primary)
- One-year PGCE (primary)
- One-year PGCE (secondary).

These courses are separate and distinct. Those undertaking them rarely, if ever, meet (other than socially) and each course has its rationale, its structure and its timetable – and they rarely overlap. Thus, although the word 'teacher' is common to both, the traditions, the emphasis and the content of the programmes differ substantially. While the Postgraduate Certificate in Education (PGCE) for those training to be primary teachers may be seen to be a conflated version of the BEd (Primary), neither of them bears much relation to the secondary course.

It is hardly surprising, therefore, that when the training is complete, the teachers who emerge regard themselves as being quite different. There has been little opportunity to discuss education generally, nor to look at the process of education from the other's perspective. Patterns of classes and teaching placements are different (for good, solid logistical reasons) and there are few opportunities even for tutors from primary and secondary courses to meet and discuss issues. On rare occasions, a perspective from one sector will be introduced to the other course through a lecture, but given the crowded nature of the curriculum, and the need to cover as much as possible within each, separate course, even these opportunities have been disappearing in recent years.

The irony is that, since the publication of *A Teaching Profession for the 21st Century* (2001), the continuation of teacher education into the first, probationary year where teachers have only a 0.7 teaching commitment to enable the local authority to provide in-service training, or continuous professional development (CPD), is often done with primary and secondary teachers together. The irony is even greater when some of the CPD is provided by staff from initial teacher education institutions who find themselves, for the first time, meeting former students from primary and secondary courses in the same place.

As Cumming (1996) points out, when the B.Ed became the main route to primary teaching in the mid 1980s, there was an attempt made to make the course 'professionally relevant'; in so doing the staffing of the course was broadened so that staff from education and psychology worked alongside primary education staff. The box below gives a breakdown of the B.Ed course content.

The content of the new B.Ed

Induction and professional studies	21 units
School experience	121 days
Curricular studies *	30 units
Elective studies	17 units

* Language and communication, mathematics for the primary school, the environment (social and scientific), expressive arts and health education.

(Cumming, p. 102)

In the early 1980s, PGCE secondary courses were evaluated by the General Teaching Council (GTC) and a set of National Guidelines produced. Kirk (1996) describes the revised guidelines which emerged in 1985:

Summary of the National Guidelines

- The specialist nature of the training was confirmed.
- The length of the programme was extended from 32 weeks to 36 weeks, and not less than 50 per cent of the programme had to be devoted to school experience.
- The partnership principle was affirmed by stipulating that school experience had to be jointly planned by college, school and education authority.
- The professional studies element of the course was required to form 'a coherent programme of study explicitly concerned with the classroom and the professional needs of the teacher ... and related to the other components of the course and, in particular, to school experience.'
- The course should be validated by an external body.
- The course should be acceptable to the General Teaching Council.

(Kirk, pp. 115/116)

Thus, while the two courses have, since the 1980s, considerable areas of overlap in terms of structure and content, the students still undergo their initial teacher education separately.

The 10–14 report – a new kind of teacher?

As we have seen, the 10–14 age group had long been seen as the next major issue to be addressed, after the Munn and Dunning reports had addressed the middle years of secondary, and *The Primary Memorandum* (1966) had, apparently, revolutionised primary education. When it was published in 1986, *Education 10–14 in Scotland* proved to be both radical and controversial, and it proposed a new way of addressing the divide between primary and secondary initial teacher education, at least for pupils at the transition stage.

The section of the report *Education 10–14 in Scotland* which looked at 'Some major implications for the educational system:

Teacher education and teaching qualifications' began with a clear statement of principle:

> Our Report is built on the belief that there are concerns of teachers and needs of children which are common to P6–P7 and to S1–S2, and therefore the attempt to achieve continuity and progression in Education 10-14 is central.
>
> *(Education 10–14 in Scotland*, 13.1)

Thus the 'concerns of teachers' and 'the needs of children' are inextricably linked in the minds of the report's authors and the principles of 'continuity and progression', later to re-emerge in the 5–14 programme, are the goal. This one sentence is indicative of the both the style and the tenor of the report; the possessive pronoun and the capital letters of 'Our Report' signals the commitment of the members of the Programme Directing Committee to the arguments and ideals outlines in the document. *Education 10–14 in Scotland* is still regarded by many educationists as one of the most enlightened reports in the modern age, certainly since the *Advisory Council Report* of 1946, a similarly progressive and well-written report which also failed to be implemented!

Education 10–14 in Scotland did not recommend middle schools ('in recognition of the realities as we perceive them' 13.2) but rather argued that 'there is a need for teachers with middle school skills, attitudes and insights.' (13.2). The report recognised that such a view would bring it into 'conflict with existing regulations for teacher qualifications' but urged upon 'Colleges of Education the need to be imaginative and so far as possible flexible' in helping to solve the problems of curriculum content at the 10–14 stage. The key to this for the report's authors was the different attitudes to teaching which they felt were inculcated in young teachers by the traditional primary and secondary courses. They singled out the secondary PGCE sector and suggested that if there were a 10–14 qualification open to both primary and secondary teachers then the latter might develop:

> ...an attitude to their own subject specialisms which sees these as only part of a broad learning fabric to which all other teachers must contribute in a cooperative way.
>
> *(ibid*, 13.3)

The 'fabric' metaphor harks back to the 'seamless robe' of the curriculum advances in 1965 by *The Primary Memorandum*. The idea of co-operation among teachers in a way which challenged the hegemony of specialisms was bound to be controversial, not only with secondary teachers but also with the General Teaching Council.

The report was advocating the coming together of teachers from primary and secondary not simply as a structural solution to the problems of discontinuity at the transition stage. Earlier in the report, a new 'curriculum design'; see below.

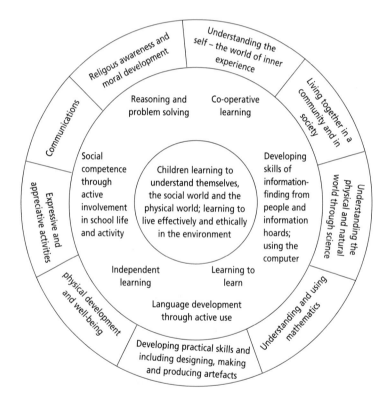

However, the report argued that these nine 'aspects of experience' were not to be confused with traditional 'subjects'. The argument was that:

> If in training the young teacher merely hears about such concepts and is never brought to experience them in the training process

itself, there is little prospect of their informing later classroom practice.

(ibid, 13.7)

The authors were not unaware of the far-reaching implications of such recommendations and acknowledged from the outset that 'there are profound implications for the organisation and allocation of college resources, both human and material' (13.7) and admitted that:

> We would be dishonest, however, to ignore the practical difficulties for the Colleges, especially those which stem from the existing patterns and structures for teacher qualifications.
>
> *(ibid*, 13.8)

The report rehearsed some of the history of teaching qualifications outlined in Chapter 2. It pointed to *The Primary Memorandum* with its insistence on primary education as a stage in its own right and to some of the early Comprehensive Education Circulars with their 'new start' philosophy as contributing to the problem, and suggested, bluntly, that 'Separation is embedded deeply in the teachers' attitudes.' (13.12). It suggested a perceived threat:

> ...to primary teachers who fear an imposition of secondary patterns and procedures, to secondary teachers who fear that their subject expertise may be undervalued and subordinated to an ill-defined 'child-centred' philosophy.
>
> *(ibid*, 13.12)

The mid-1980s was a period of falling school rolls and teachers were suspicious of any change which might be motivated more by economic or political rather than educational reasons.

However, there were more prosaic obstacles to the fulfilment of the report's ideal. In 1982, the GTC had made it impossible for any holder of a secondary teaching qualification to teach general subjects in primary schools, and was less than enthusiastic when Colleges proposed courses which led to dual qualifications. The report considered each of the existing routes to teaching qualification – the four-year B.Ed and the one-year PGCE in primary or in secondary education – and acknowledged that change would be difficult, and unwelcome. Indeed, the report recognised that qualifications which would lead to 'free movement to teach across the boundary' were a long way away – 'History is against it and the climate is wrong.' (13.16).

In-service training – 'better solutions'?

At any one time, there are many more teachers in post than there are in training, and the report acknowledged that in-service rather than pre-service training might provide 'better solutions'. At the time, there were in-service BEds available to teachers already qualified in primary, and there were associateships, including one in upper primary (8–12). It was suggested that:

> ...a way forward for 10–14 developments through the extension of associateship-type courses must be a reasonable long-term prospect. As special qualifications they would confer some strength and credibility on teachers involved across the 10–14 range, from P6 to S2, without changing the basic category of teaching qualification.'
>
> (*ibid*, 13.17)

This pragmatism was admirable but temporary. In a report destined to be regarded as too radical by the incoming Conservative Minister for Education, Michael Forsyth, 'a different approach' was proposed:

> We believe that the way ahead is not through trying to turn primary teachers into secondary teachers and vice versa.
>
> (*ibid*, 13.17)

The report looked at existing Advanced Diploma courses available in guidance and in learning difficulties, both aimed at secondary teachers, and concluded that there 'was no compelling reason why such an Advanced Diploma should not be open to all teachers as a mark of continued professional development.' It suggested that:

> One module could relate to the rationale for the curriculum at 10–14, another might look at personal growth and social education over the same age range. Yet another might examine assessment and recording techniques.
>
> (*ibid*, 13.17)

The idea was that local authorities would nominate teachers to these courses 'if they believed in 10–14 continuity' and saw the prime initial candidates as being Assistant headteachers in upper primary and lower secondary schools. With a final, unwittingly ironic, nod in the direction of the financial implications of such a proposal, the report stated:

> the outlay would be small for such a potentially valuable return to so many pupils.
>
> (*ibid*, 13.17)

Teachers - part of the problem or part of the solution?

In the event, none of the report's 100 or so recommendations was implemented. The 5–14 programme was set in motion before the ink was dry on the 10–14 report, and the rest is history. However, the lessons learned may still be important. The 10–14 report was philosophically teacher-centred, in the tradition of *The Primary Memorandum*. However, by the time the report was concluded, the teaching profession had been through a period of protracted and often bitter industrial action, where one of the tactics had been to withdraw from curriculum development. Standard Grade implementation had been a temporary casualty of the action, and Ministers in the Scottish Office were experiencing a sense of frustration with the profession.

The consultation paper *Curriculum and Assessment: a Policy for the 90s* which was in preparation before the 10–14 report's authors were aware of the new political climate in the Scottish Office, has been described by Roger and Hartley (1990) as 'the epitaph ... of progressive primary education' (p. 103). The paper threatened local authorities with legislation if, for example, National Testing was not carried out. The 5–14 programme was to be more direct and quicker than the evolutionary approach of the 10–14 report. External controls in the form of levels and testing would replace the 'autonomy within guidelines' of 10–14. Bill Gatherer (1989) has referred to this as a 'new authoritarianism'. The tide was certainly turning.

The new approach to policy-making characterised by Michael Forsyth in the Scottish Office was based on a lack of trust in the teaching profession. This, in turn, was exemplified by the 5–14 model of central control rather than the traditional partnership which was at the heart of Scottish education. Bruce Milan, a former Secretary of State for Education, had famously said:

> I think at the end of the day the system does change, and change significantly, but it just can't be done by administrative or Ministerial fiat, you know. It just doesn't work like that.
>
> (*Governing Education*, 1988, p. ix)

– unless you are Michael Forsyth, that is, and a Secretary of State in Mrs Thatcher's Government!

Thus, the model was changing. Traditionally, the Scottish approach was high on teacher autonomy and high on partnership. Now, post 10–14, we saw a move to a model which was high on centralism and high on compulsion.

National Initiatives and the policy dimensions

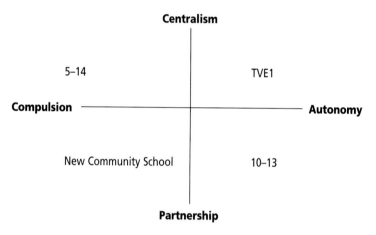

The figure above shows the 10–14 and 5–14 approaches in terms of their philosophical starting point, with two other developments to complete the picture. Thus, 10–14 would have been high on partnership and high on autonomy while 5–14 was, in terms of the Minister's view, high on centralism and high on compulsion. On the other hand, TVEI was centralist in origin while leaving room for local autonomy, while new community schools are compulsory in that all authorities have to have them, but there is a partnership model which includes the sharing of good practice and evidence from evaluation

The key question in 1986/87, was would teachers respond to the imposition of a centralist model of the curriculum? Did their existing practice really merit such lack of ministerial trust? Were they really part of the problem? The imposition of levels of attainment, of national testing and of guidelines on every subject area, later to be reinforced by targets, was a long way from *The Primary Memorandum* and a long way from the 10–14 report. In the interests of breadth, balance, continuity, coherence and progression, existing levels of teacher and school autonomy were to be constrained. The Guidelines were to become mandatory, if not, as in England and Wales, statutory. The age of the 'integrated day' and the 'seamless robe' of the curriculum were to be sacrificed on the altar of 'standards'.

Making the best of 5–14

While members of the 10–14 committee felt betrayed that their report had been, as they saw it, hijacked, by the New Right, they nevertheless, in the tradition of Scottish Education, set about making sure that 5–14 would be as good as it could be. Gordon Liddell, a stalwart of the Consultative Committee on the Curriculum and a member of the Review and Development Committee on English Language 5–14 saw RGD 1, as it came to be known, as: '... a damage limitation exercise, but now I think that our group feels that some considerable good may come out of it. Its report will be published intact...'.

David Robertson, the chair of the 10–14 committee was just as sanguine: '5–14 will work fine. People are sensible enough. Bill Gatherer, formerly a senior figure in the Inspectorate, echoed these sentiments: '... I have an abiding faith in the integrity of educators ... ultimately schools will overcome various types of attack.' (Boyd, 1993 p. 286)

Sir James Munn made a similar point about TVEI: '..[it] has been triumphantly successful in my view. I mean the process of taking what were raw political notions and turning them into sound educational notions.' (Boyd, p. 287)

Sydney Smyth summed up this line of argument when he said:

> I think that the RDGs are, particularly in the concept of the strand, producing a rationale, You can weave the strands together into a kind of seamless robe of learning which was the Memorandum's favourite epistemological metaphor. I maintain it could actually improve the quality of education in primary schools. I'm not as pessimistic at that level. In fact, I'm optimistic.' (*Boyd*, p. 287)

However optimistic Smyth was, there was to be a very public battle fought over what some saw as the heart of the matter.

Testing was the symbolic rubicon which those concerned about 5–14's centralism would not cross. It began as 'primary testing' at ages four and seven, a kind of 'benchmarking' where all pupils would sit tests in English and maths within a six-week window around Easter each year. However to many people, from large local authorities like Strathclyde to parents groups nationally and locally, this was a step too far. It smacked of the Qualifying Examination ('the Quali' in the vernacular) – Scotland's Eleven Plus. Accusations of undue stress on young children were made and the profession saw the trust in which primary teachers had historically been held being challenged. In the face of such opposition accompanied by mass withdrawals by parents of their children from the tests, the Government gave way. The victory was, in some respects, phyrric. What happened was that tests remained, were extended to all five Levels of the 5–14 programme but were to be administered as and when the teacher deemed appropriate. National testing remained but the teachers' judgement was acknowledged in the process.

Thus, within a national programme which was high on centralism and high on control, national tests were compulsory, but only to be administered as and when the teacher deemed the pupil(s) to be ready. They were to be a national benchmark against which the teacher would test her/his own judgement that the child was, indeed, working consistently at a particular level. This level of teacher autonomy was not only anomalous within an otherwise centrally controlled initiative, it would prove to be one of the stumbling blocks to the success of the whole 5–14 initiative. The problem was that not only did secondary teachers question the reliability of the test results, claiming that the teacher autonomy led to inconsistency of assessment across associated primary schools, but the test results – i.e. the 5–14 levels – began to be used for purposes for which they were not designed, namely 'setting' in the secondary school.

The paradox was summed up by a principal teacher (PT) of mathematics interviewed as part of the research carried out by Boyd and Simpson (2000) in a local authority in Scotland. First of all, the PT questioned the reliability of the primary schools' application of levels, claiming that they 'were all over the place'. However, the assistant principal teacher (APT) who was also in on the interview had already argued that the department had to set by attainment at the beginning of S1 because 'you can't teach maths in mixed ability classes'. When asked what assessment information the department used therefore to set the pupils, the PT said 5–14 levels and when asked why, given his previous comments about unreliability, he replied, 'well, it's all we've got. We set them again in October, using our own test scores.'

In 2003, against a backdrop of increasing disquiet about national testing from teachers, local authorities and some parents' groups, the Minister announced a consultation exercise which would consider alternatives to national tests as well as improvements to the present system. The realisation that the same test instruments could not be used to confirm teachers' professional judgements *and* act as a device for internal selection in secondary schools had dawned at last. The Minister proposed a revised version of the Assessment of Achievement Programme, a research exercise carried out nationally on a three-year cycle, measuring the progress of a 10 per cent sample of P4. Pupils from P7 and S2 across Scotland in English, maths and science, might replace national test targets at a national level.

However, the issue of the 'fresh start' approach which the 1993 HMI report, *The Education of Able Pupils P6 to S2*, had dismissed as 'no longer tenable' remains. The 5–14 programme has brought to Scottish education a common language which primary and secondary teachers can use to discuss the curriculum, and a set of common criteria against which to measure pupil progress. It has enabled imaginative 'bridging projects' to be devised across P7 and S1 in some areas and, at best, it has promoted discussion about curriculum content across primary schools and with associated secondaries. But, it has only scratched the surface of curricular continuity, coherence and progression. The structures of the secondary curriculum have proved, in some cases, impregnable. Environmental studies sits uncomfortably across some eight or nine secondary subjects and cross-curricular coherence was always going to be a challenge in the subject-dominated secondary curriculum. Even Expressive Arts, with its more obviously cognate subjects, struggles to be seen as a coherent subject area in the secondary school. Add to this the lack of trust about assessment information which can exist between the two sectors, and it is not difficult to see why 5–14 has not been an unqualified success.

Primary–secondary transition: a suitable case for CPD?

As we have seen, historically there have been difficulties in addressing the issue of primary–secondary transition through initial teacher education. The courses which have been accredited and validated, overseen by GTC and inspected by HMIE, seem too inflexible to involve primary and secondary graduates and undergraduates working together. The in-service model, perhaps a variation on the Additional Teaching Qualification (ATQ) may prove to be a more pragmatic solution. In this way, it might be possible, in any given cluster of secondary and associated primary schools, to have a team of teachers having taken the ATQ in 10–14 Studies, who could work across the sectors. The presence of primary and secondary teachers working together could provide more specialism in the upper primary and more generalism in the lower secondary, and could lead to greater coherence across the subject areas.

However, even if this were to come to pass, it would be slow and would, of necessity, involve only a minority of teachers at any one time. How do the rest of the teachers become aware of the issues and develop the understandings and skills which will lead to greater continuity, coherence and progression in the curriculum? One answer may be continuing professional development.

If we believe that Scottish teachers have always been part of the solution, though from time to time some have seen them as part of the problem (not least at the point when the 10–14 report was published), there needs to be an investment on continuing professional development. *A Teaching Profession for the 21st Century* has signalled the importance of CPD and has, indeed, made it an entitlement for all teachers. In the context of primary–secondary liaison, more opportunities must be created to bring primary and secondary teachers together to share their expertise in learning and teaching. There should be opportunities also for those working in early years and pre-five education, and for those working with young people with additional support needs to participate jointly in such CPD. And, of course, as the new community schools and learning communities take root, there needs to be opportunity to include others who work with young people. The principle is clear: investment in CPD is investment in young people. In Chapter 8, we will look at how to achieve the greatest benefit from CPD.

Unexpected pressures for change

In 2003, the Education Minister announced that maximum class sizes in English and maths in the first two years of secondary would be reduced to 20 (from 33) within five years as part of the Government's strategy for raising levels of attainment. Although the move was met with approval in principle, the teaching profession, especially the Headteachers Association Scotland (HAS), was quick to point out that such a reduction was impracticable for two reasons; firstly, there were not enough graduates applying for initial teacher education to bring about the increase in the teaching force required, and, secondly, in those schools which were already full, there were simply not enough classrooms to accommodate the increase number of classes which would be created.

The second of these two problems will have to be solved by local authorities as a building or accommodation matter, and may actually increase the pressure on already over-subscribed schools. The first is being taken up by the ITE universities, and in at least one, Strathclyde, there are discussions taking place with a view to revisiting the 10–14 report's idea of a P6 to S2 teacher. The idea would be to address two issues, namely recruiting more maths teachers by retraining existing teachers while at the same time looking at the possibility, through an ATQ addressing the problems of continuity and progression.

In addition, the McCrone settlement, *A Teaching Profession for the 21st Century*, put pressure on the system by guaranteeing all primary teachers a minimum of two hours and 30 minutes non-contact time each week. The obvious question was how to free up teachers while causing the minimum disruption to the continuity of the pupils' learning.

On 5 December 2003, the Times Educational Supplement Scotland ran a feature under the headline *Special Branch*, which highlighted an approach being taken in a cluster of schools within the Highland region. The report began:

> An engineer, a Francophile, an information technology expert and a ballet dancer are helping Highland education authority to solve a problem arising from the national teachers' agreement.

The most notable aspect of this initiative was that these four were primary teachers, not 'specialists' from the secondary. In fact, *they* were the specialists, and what is more, they worked across all of the primaries involved. So far, there is no suggestion that these specialists would work in the secondaries also, as part of an inter-disciplinary or cross-sectoral team, but it is as close to the concept of the 10–14 teacher as we have seen to date in Scotland. The danger highlighted by some of the staff is that these specialisms are being removed from the remit of the class teachers and de-skilling could result. Nevertheless, the specialist–generalist divide between secondary and primary schools is being challenged.

SUMMARY

Historically, primary and secondary teachers have been trained separately, even when in the same institution. The ITE courses have many points of overlap, but the student teachers rarely, if ever, come together. The 10–14 report identified this as an issue and while mindful of the structural obstacles, nevertheless recommended a coming together of primary and secondary in ITE, in is-service training and through other, more imaginative, means. The 10–14 report was never implemented, falling foul of the new right agenda of a Michael Forsyth-led Scottish Office intent on imposing a new, more centralist approach to policy-making on Scottish education. For the profession, the early days of 5–14 became a damage limitation exercise. One possibility is that the recent Scottish Executive pledge to reduce class size in English and maths in S1 and S2 has once again focused attention on this area and may be the catalyst for a reconsideration of the concept of a 10–14 teacher.

POINTS FOR REFLECTION

1   Is it possible to create a middle school concept without building middle schools? Is it desirable?

2   Is the idea of an ATQ to develop a cadre of 10–14 teachers, working across the sectors in teams, likely to find favour with the profession, with the GTC, with the teaching unions, with parents and with pupils?

3   What are the barriers to and benefits of joint CPD with primary and secondary teachers looking at continuity, coherence and continuity?

4 How do children learn?

> 'Rabbit's clever,' said Pooh thoughtfully.
> 'Yes,' said Piglet, 'Rabbit's clever.
> 'And he has a brain'
> 'Yes,' said Piglet, 'Rabbit has a brain.'
> There was a long silence.
> 'I suppose,' said Pooh, 'that that's why he never understands anything.'
>
> *Winnie the Pooh*, **A. A. Milne**

The learning brain

Ian Smith (2000) has suggested that the 1990s were the 'decade of the brain' since it has been claimed that some 90 per cent of what we currently know about the brain and how we learn was discovered during that period. Hannaford (1995) and Buzan (2001) have reminded us, however, that learning does not simply involve the brain but involves the whole body. *Mens sana in corpore sano* (a healthy mind in a healthy body) may have been around for a long time as a slogan, but it is as true today as it was in Roman times. Gardner (1993) and, more recently, Goleman (1996) have changed our views on the concept of 'intelligence', de-bunking the myth that it is somehow a single entity, inherited, fixed and predictable over time. Add to this the growing evidence from cognitive research that we all have preferred 'learning styles', whether auditory, visual or kinaesthetic, and we begin to appreciate both the complexity of the learning process itself but also the possibility that teachers can help all learners to find a way to be successful. Gardner has invited us to consider his eight different intelligences as 'entry points' into the learning process. Feuerstein has suggested that if a child appears unable to learn something, do not assume that the child is unintelligent; rather assume that child's intelligence is 'lying dormant'.

When Roger Sperry's Nobel prize-winning work on 'left brain, right brain' was published in 1968, it seemed to have little immediate relevance to the average classroom. It was not until the late 1980s, when Levy (1988) drew together all the research, that the potential impact began to become clear. Thus while it is true to say that our brain has two hemispheres and that each has distinct functions, both sides of the brain are used in almost every human activity. Indeed, Jensen (1995) suggests:

> Use the two sides as a metaphor for understanding how we process instead of pigeon-holing all behaviours into either left or right brain.
>
> (p. 4)

Jensen is reminding us, if we need reminding, that the brain is hugely complex and we know that it can operate on many different levels as well as being what Buzan refers to as 'synergetic', namely that the brain 'multiplies' by making connections. It is not a simple adding machine, taking each thought or piece of information and storing it. Its potential is, in a real sense, infinite.

Left brain	Right brain
Words	Rhythm
Logic	Spatial awareness
Numbers	Dimension
Sequence	Imagination
Linearity	Daydreaming
Analysis	Colour
Lists	Gestalt
	(in Buzan 2000)

It is certainly true that now, in the twenty-first century, teachers are applying more of what they know about how human beings learn, to their work in the classroom. There is no shortage of advice to help them in this task; the challenge is to make sense of the ever-growing mountain of books on learning so that this 'new knowledge' can be applied.

The importance of intelligence

In his typically whimsical manner, Pooh reminds us that the relationship between being 'clever', having a brain and understanding things, is not quite as simple as it seems. Indeed the very word, 'clever', is a good starting point in the quest to find out how young people learn. In our Western society, being clever is a highly valued commodity. For more than a century, we have tried to measure this thing called 'intelligence'. The psychometricians of the early twentieth century devised new and more sophisticated tests of what became known as IQ – Intelligence Quotient. Whether it be verbal or non-verbal, mathematical or spatial, it seemed that these tests, with their national norms and their basis in psychology, offered a simple and robust measure of every human being's 'intelligence'.

The present writer had his IQ measured, along with his classmates in the 1950s, on two occasions while at primary school. Along with the qualifying examination, they had been used up until the late 1950s to select pupils for different kinds of school: junior secondary for the non-academic; senior secondary for the academic. The 'average' IQ was 100, and those pupils who scored below 70 were deemed to be suitable for 'special education'. For those whose scores were in the 120+ category, a university education beckoned.

As late as the mid-1970s, when the present writer was teaching in a Renfrewshire junior high school, IQ still had a part to play in selection. All of the pupils from the associated primary schools came to our junior high school. At the end of their second year in the school, each principal teacher had to predict which pupils were capable of achieving a Higher pass in that subject, three years later. Without dwelling on the validity of such a process, it must be said that teachers tended to give pupils the benefit of the doubt. Every year, too many pupils were deemed capable of three or more Highers than the senior high school could, or would, take. Thus, the headteacher looked at IQ scores. Those in the 120+ bracket were certainties. Those between 100 and 120 were possibilities. Those below 100 had clearly 'peaked', were over-performing and did not go to the senior high school. A generation earlier in England and Wales, pass marks in the Eleven Plus exams were routinely lowered for boys so as to achieve a gender balance. In the early 1900s, the Stanford-Binet test scores for women were deliberately lowered by removing the items in which women had outscored men.

Another influence of IQ at the same school was the grading of pupils according to the 'normal curve of distribution'. The theory was that if everyone in the world where tested using the same IQ test, the scores would form a normal curve in the ratio 1:2:4:2:1. Thus there would be a top 10 per cent well above average; 20 per cent above average; 40 per cent average; 20 per cent below average; and 10 per cent well below average. When the scores in each subject were counted for pupils in the first and second year, the pupils were ranked in order and they were awarded grades according to the normal curve ratio. Thus, 10 per cent were awarded As; 20 per cent, Bs; 40 per cent, Cs; 20 per cent, Ds and 10 per cent, Es. The questionable assumption that this distribution was valid, was further threatened when the sample size was only 200 or so. It was when the suggestion was made that the ratio applied also to a mixed ability class of 30 pupils, that the practice was finally questioned and then abandoned.

The history of IQ has been dogged by controversy, not least when Herrnstein and Murray in their controversial book, *The Bell Curve* (1994) argued that there was a racial element to IQ and that white Caucasians had higher IQs on average than black African and African–Americans. *The Bell Curve* sold more copies than any other social scientific book of its time and re-opened the debate on intelligence and race which had been raised in Jensen's article, *How Much Can We Boost IQ and Scholastic Achievemement?* in 1969. Thus, when Howard Gardner advanced his theory of multiple intelligences, it challenged many long-held assumptions and changed forever the way we speak about intelligence. Gardner suggests that we can no longer ask the question 'how smart are you?' and that the only legitimate question is 'how are you smart?'

Intelligences	Definition
Linguistic	A facility with language, patterning and systems
Logical/mathematical thinking	Likes precision and enjoys abstract and structural
Musical	Sensitive to mood and emotion, enjoys rhythm, understands complex organisation of music
Visual/Spatial	Thinks in pictures and mental images, good with maps, charts and diagrams, uses movement to assist learning

Kinaesthetic	Good timing, skilled at handicrafts, likes to act and touch, good control of objects
Interpersonal	Relates well to others, mediator, good communicator
Intrapersonal	Self-motivated, high degree of self knowledge, strong sense of values
Naturalistic	Empathy with the natural world, perceptive about the environment, sense of how things inter-relate

(Howard Gardner)

The implications of Gardner's work for schools have emerged over the years since his theory became public knowledge, and are, potentially, huge. Practices which have existed since time immemorial and which have been promoted by august bodies such as HMIE, such as 'setting' by ability or by prior attainment become distinctly questionable. In other words, if a child appears unable to make progress in a subject or area of the curriculum, the response should not be to assume that s/he cannot learn the particular concept of set of ideas. Rather the challenge should be to find the correct 'entry point', either, as Gardner would suggest, through another intelligence, or as Goleman would suggest, by focusing on an aspect of the learner's 'emotional intelligence' to re-engage the learner.

In other words, labelling learners or seeking to put them into categories which might limit their aspirations, as well as limiting the expectations of their teachers, should be avoided. In the present context, the 5–14 levels (A to F) should not be used as judgements to sort pupils out, but as broad indicators of the level of current performance of the individual pupil. Any assessment which takes place in the context of the learning environment, usually a classroom, should be *formative*, i.e., it should have as its main purpose the improvement of the child's present and future learning. This feedback should focus on the steps the learner has to take to become better at the task in which s/he is engaged. More importantly, if we want the child to become an independent learner we have to share the 'quality criteria' against which the learning will be assessed and we need to give the learner the skills needed for self assessment. This notion of 'learning to learn', or *metacognition*, is fundamental to the learning process and transcends historical notions of intelligence; it is central to the Scottish Executive's initiative, *Assessment is for Learning.*

For too long, intelligence has been a distraction in terms of looking at why it is that some pupils fail to achieve or to make satisfactory progress in learning. It has been too easy to explain away such instances by saying 'well, he's not very bright'. When, in late August 1970, the pupil (in class 3m 2 boys at a junior secondary school) faced with a lesson on Wilfred Owen's poem *Dulce et decorum est*, said to the young teacher, 'sir, we don't do this kind of stuff; we're thick', he had simply internalised the messages which the system had sent out by placing him in the lowest class in third year in a school for 'non-academic' pupils. The fact that he had intervened to try to make contact with the teacher, to offer a truce and to suggest an accommodation until he and his fellow pupils left school at Christmas, may well indicate that he had what we now recognise as high levels of 'emotional intelligence'. But, in 1970, he was simply regarded as a 'slow learner'.

Intelligence and creativity

There has long been a controversy about the relationship between intelligence and creativity. Getzels and Jackson (1962) conducted a study with pupils in a private school in Chicago whose average IQ was 130. Later, in 1964, Kogan and Wallach conducted a similar study on pupils with low measured IQs. The aim in both cased was to find out the relationship between intelligence and creativity. Their results were interesting.

Intelligence and creativity

High creativity – high intelligence
These children can exercise within themselves both control and freedom, both adult-like and childlike kinds of behaviour.

High creativity – low intelligence
These children are in angry conflict with themselves and with their school environment and are beset by feelings unworthiness and inadequacy. In a stress-free context, however, they can blossom cognitively.

Low creativity – high intelligence
These children can be described as addicted to the school environment. Academic failure would be conceived by them as catastrophic, so that they must continually strive for academic excellence in order to avoid the possibility of pain.

Low creativity – low intelligence
Basically bewildered, these children engaged in various defensive manoeuvres ranging from useful adaptations such as intensive social activity to regressions such as passivity or psychosomatic symptoms.

(Young and Tyre, *Gifted or Able?* 1992)

Bearing in mind the problematic nature of the concept of intelligence, this analysis suggests that the needs of three-quarters of the pupil population at any given time are not being met. However, there is a question mark over both sets of tests used in these studies and it is doubtful if all children easily fit into any one of these categories.

Emotional intelligence

In his book *Emotional Intelligence* (1996) Daniel Goleman takes the issue of intelligence a stage further. Gardner, as we have seen, had already identified two intelligences which he called *interpersonal* and *intrapersonal*. Goleman takes these two and, in trying to answer the question why it is that IQ has always been a relatively poor indicator of future success, suggests that a whole set of attributes including self-control, zeal, persistence and ability to motivate oneself, might offer a better way of predicting future success. Indeed, he questions Gardner's view of the moral neutrality of intelligence, and argues that restraint rather than impulsivity, and empathy rather than selfishness, are desirable moral attributes.

In the context of the move from primary to secondary, is there any evidence that the emotional development of young people plays a significant part in their ability to learn? Goleman suggests that we can be taught to improve our emotional intelligence. He proposes that schools should teach very young children 'basic lessons in self-awareness, relationships and decision-making' (p. 275). Many primary schools do this already through personal and social development. In some cases, specific approaches are used such as *circle time* (Mosley) or *philosophy for children* (Lipman). In others, there may be *stories for thinking* (Fisher) or programmes such as *new haven* which Goleman features in his book. In the new haven programme, the children, as they reach the later stages of primary, are taught such strategies as 'impulse control, empathy and even anger management'. By the time they move into secondary school, Goleman would suggest that pupils should be taught how to deal with the various temptations life can throw at them, as well as how to look at problems through different perspectives, with an emphasis on empathy.

There is clearly an issue about the impact of the move to secondary school on the emotional development of young people. The safe, secure environment of the primary school, with a single teacher, one classroom and very highly developed routines, rules and responsibilities changes, over a six-week period, to a large complex institution, with as many as fifteen different teachers in a week, each in his/her own classroom and with hundreds of fellow pupils, almost all of them older than the new first years. If systems are not in place to make the transition smooth, there is real danger that the experience could be an emotionally negative one.

Ages and stages

It has long been argued that children develop as learners in predictable stages. The work of Jean Piaget was highly influential in this regard, particularly in the way which it influenced *The Primary Memorandum* (1966). This ground-breaking official document produced by the SED was to transform thinking about primary education in Scotland. It was in many respects, a watershed in Scottish primary education and is widely attributed with the move to child-centeredness, activity methods and the application of Piaget's theories to the learning and teaching process. Indeed a commentator of the time, Osborne, remarked that the Scottish education department seemed to subscribe to the work of Piaget 'with all the appearance of having undergone a sudden conversion.' Paradoxically, Piaget's name does not appear in the index of *The Primary Memorandum*, but his ideas permeate the report.

A singular contribution of *The Primary Memorandum* was in its claim that primary education should be viewed as having equal status with secondary:

> it is now generally accepted that the primary school is much more than a preparation for the secondary school; it is a stage of development in its own right.
>
> (p. 3)

Gatherer has argued (1989) that *The Primary Memorandum* ranks alongside the Plowden report of 1967 as one of highest expressions of the 'progressive movement' in education in Great Britain:

> its principle tenets – that each child should be allowed to progress at her or his appropriate pace, that the school should cater for individual needs and capacities, that specific knowledge is less important than the fostering of learning skills and the capacity to acquire knowledge independently – soon came to be adopted as received wisdom by British professional educators.
>
> (p. 69)

The Primary Memorandum was not without its difficulties, however. The freedom given by it to teachers was a challenge to their established roles within the classroom. Gatherer observed:

> But the new emphasis on the class teacher's role was more problematical. The essential point is that the modern primary curriculum is creatively managed by the teacher in the process of arousing the children's interest and learning needs. Thus the teacher should decide, albeit under guidance, what the pupils should study, what skills should be taught in particular contexts and what kind of learning strategies should be aimed for in any given classroom activity.
>
> (p. 67/68)

Some 40 years later, in 2003, the Department for Education and Skills (DfES) published *Education and Excellence*, which outlined, after three decades of highly centralised curriculum directives enshrined in the National Curriculum, 'Existing and planned freedoms' for teachers:

Existing and planned freedoms

Within the curriculum, teachers and schools have the freedom to decide:

How to teach – the programmes of study state in outline what is to be taught, but not how it is to be taught. Schemes of work are an optional tool – schools can ignore them, adapt them, or pick and choose between [sic] them. The National Literacy and Numeracy Strategies, though they are supported strongly, are not statutory and can be adapted to meet schools' particular needs. Ofsted will welcome and recognise good practice.

Which aspects of a subject pupils will study in depth – the requirement is that schools cover the programme of study, but it is for individual teachers to decide which aspects they wish to emphasise. For example, they may choose to cover some aspects in a single afternoon, and turn others into work lasting a whole term.

How long to spend on each subject – It is for schools to decide how they are going to organise their timetable. Qualifications and Curriculum Authority (QCA) guidance suggesting how much time should be allocated to each subject is not statutory.

How to arrange learning in the school day – there is no requirement for subjects to be taught discreetly – they can be grouped, or taught through projects. If strong enough links are created between subjects, pupils' knowledge and skills can be used across the whole curriculum.

To use sections of previous or later programmes of study – some pupils' learning needs will be better matched by programmes of study from earlier or later Key Stages.

(*Excellence and Enjoyment* pp. 16/17)

The concept of stages has been interpreted too literally for many educational theorists and practitioners since Piaget's work was published. In the 1960s, Bruner extended the idea of stages and of 'discovery learning' proposed by Piaget and introduced the idea of 'active ratiocination', or thinking for yourself. Discovery learning was all very well, but it had to be guided by someone, usually a teacher. For Bruner, learners have to know where they are going and to have some basic concepts in order to make sense of their experiences.

Vygotsky, writing in the early part of the twentieth century, saw learning as an active process. Like Piaget, he believed that human beings construct knowledge as a result of their interaction with others, their social surroundings and the wider world. 'The thinking child is the social child' said Vygotsky, and his metaphor of 'scaffolding' described how as learners become increasingly independent, the teacher can remove the scaffolding or support systems. The statement 'What the child can do in collaboration with others today, he can do by himself tomorrow', sums up the importance Vygotsky placed on interaction, discussion and making sense of new knowledge by relating it to prior learning. Thus the deterministic element of Piaget's theory was refined, and social constructivism became a powerful way of describing the learning process. Essentially, Piaget's notion of discovery learning was developed by Vygotsky who stressed the role of guided learning, arguing that the 'zone of proximal development' is:

> The distance between the actual development of the child as determined by independent problem-solving under adult guidance or in collaboration with more capable peers.
>
> (*Thought and Language*, p. 86)

Put simply, the Zone of Proximal Development (ZPD) is the gap between the most difficult task the child can accomplish independently and the most difficult task s/he can accomplish with assistance. Getting from one to the other, for Vygotsky, is a collaborative enterprise.

In the United States in the 1960s, Matthew Lipman developed an approach which became known as the 'community or enquiry' or 'philosophy for children'. Lipman, building on the work of Vygotsky, believed that very young children were capable of abstract reasoning provided that there was a framework within which they could operate. Lipman argued that the narrative or storytelling framework was a powerful one, and he wrote a number of novellas in which concepts such as love, fear, respect, trust, betrayal, loyalty, etc. were explored within a story aimed at children as young as five or six years of age. Indeed, one of his students, Catherine McCall, introduced his approach into Scottish primary schools in the 1990s and made a video of the process, entitled 'Socrates for six year olds'!

At the same time, the approach called 'circle time' was being introduced into primary schools in England and Wales by Jenny

Mosley, based on a similar principle, namely that young children could interact socially and intellectually at a very much earlier age than Piaget seemed to suggest. In the 1990s, the notion of stages being fixed and predictable for all children was being challenged, and with it assumptions about they could and could not learn. The irony was that the 5–14 programme seemed to be operating on a Piagetian set of assumptions about levels and stages which were at odds with the newer ways of thinking.

Making learning continuous, progressive and coherent

The challenge for primary and secondary schools is to use the new research into how human beings learn, in order to ensure that learning from P6 to S2 (and beyond) is continuous, progressive and coherent. While most teachers do not consciously adhere to particular theories of learning, there is evidence that part of the problem of transition from primary to secondary may reside in the different ways in which teachers in the two sectors conceptualise the learning and teaching process.

In the primary school, the approach is still heavily influenced by a set of theories which have elements of Piaget, Vygotsky, Bruner and, in recent years, have elements of thinking skills, influenced by Robert Fisher's work and his distillation of the ideas of Lipman, Feuerstein, De Bono and others. Group work is heavily used in primary classrooms, the teacher often sees herself as a *facilitator* and *guide* to pupils' learning, and connections are made between learning in one part of the curriculum and learning in another.

In the secondary school, it is more likely that teachers have in mind a *transmission* model where the teacher is the 'expert' and the learner is the 'apprentice'. In the 1980s and 1990s in Scotland, HMI seemed to reinforce such a view with their advice to teachers, particularly in secondary schools, to use Direct Teaching, later re-presented as Direct Interactive Teaching. Concerned about 'pace of learning', an ill-defined concept which seemed to suggest that good learning was fast learning, HMI were unhappy about group work, especially where there were different activities taking place. The same concern was being expressed in England and Wales by Ofsted, where Chris Woodhead, HMSCI, was openly critical of 'woolly' theories of learning. Thus secondary teachers were being urged towards more didactic approaches in order to increase the pace of learning.

At the same time, in the 1980s and 1990s, secondary schools were being advised to 'set' pupils by prior attainment, based on 5–14 levels or on standardised tests, or both, in order to ensure that 'pace of learning' would be appropriate and that attainment would be raised. No such pressure was put on primary schools at this stage, though it would come later. The effect of such pressure was to emphasise further the role of teacher-led, didactic teaching in the secondary school. Group work began to decline, discussion was seen as a luxury and the pressure was on to 'get through the curriculum'.

Meanwhile, the traditional idea of the 'integrated day' in the primary schools, although in practice more mythical than real, was consigned to the dustbin of history as the 5–14 programme began to impose a tight timetable structure on primary schools. The balance of time across the curricular areas had to be met, and primary headteachers had to timetable more rigidly than ever before. Thus, while there was no Literacy Hour or Numeracy Hour as in England and Wales, there emerged a *de facto* hour of language and of number each morning for just about every primary school pupil in Scotland. The holistic approach to learning which was seen as the hallmark of primary schools, began to crumble in the attempt to cover all of the elements of the curriculum Even environmental studies, a holistic approach to science, social subjects and technology, was sub-divided into its constituent parts in 2002, in the light of concerns that it was too 'amorphous'.

Learning to think; thinking to learn

Dr Margaret Kirkwood's book in this CPD series, *Learning to Think; Thinking to Learn* (2005), outlines the history, the theoretical basis and the developing practice of thinking skills. It may be that thinking skills can offer a bridge between the learning which takes place in primary and secondary schools in Scotland. My contention is that the 5–14 programme has failed in its central aims of improving attainment (originally, it was suggested, to such an extent that Standard Grade could be moved to S3) and establishing continuity and progression in pupils' learning in the late primary and early secondary stages. Simply calling the programme 5–14 was never going to guarantee that the two sectors would come closer together in terms of learning. It is not that schools and local authorities have been reluctant to put in the effort. As we have seen, there are numerous examples of good practice in trying to join up the learning process. But, as Boyd and Simpson found (2000), almost all of the successes were in the area of pastoral care, additional support needs, aligning curriculum content and smoothing the transition from P7 to S1. Progression and continuity in learning and teaching remains a distant dream for many primary staff, a nightmare for some secondary staff and an area of limited success in most parts of the country.

However, there is hope. The review of the curriculum 3–18 may pave the way for greater continuity and progression. Joining up the initiatives, from *Assessment is for Learning* to *Better behaviour; better learning* is another. A third possibility is taking a thinking skills perspective and looking at how teachers and others involved in children's learning can promote thinking in all aspects of learning with the goal of *metacognition* being the unifying factor. In a recent address on the subject of thinking skills, Professor Carol McGuinness of Queen's University, Belfast argued that 'education for thinking' was what was required in the twenty-first century. Her contention was that 'good thinking does not emerge spontaneously' but needs explicit guidance and instruction. Drawing on a body of research, much of which has already been cited in this volume, she suggested that:

- Active cognitive processing makes for better learning.
- Being explicit about thinking and educating directly for it works best.
- A focus on creating challenges and higher order thinking is necessary.
- Thinking is effortful.

Her view was that for too much of the time in primary and in secondary schools, the thinking children are asked to do is routine and mundane. She advocated 'nuanced thinking' and tasks that need multiple solution, which involve uncertainty and in which learners need to impose meaning on the situation; thus, making thinking 'visible' in the classroom, talking about thinking, employing strategies which encourage thinking, using knowledge to promote thinking (not stifle it) and, above all, creating 'dispositions for thinking'. It is this latter point which may offer the key to successful learning from P6 to S2.

Professor McGuinness argued that thinking is 'a will as well as a skill'. In other words, we need to help pupils to become well disposed to thinking, to see it as a natural part of learning. Pupils need to be given the *vocabulary* of thinking, and to be supported and directed to become better thinkers and better learners. Thus, as South Lanarkshire and others, have tried to do, teachers need access to high quality thinking skills programmes and, most importantly, to high quality CPD so that they are confident about promoting thinking in their classrooms. Progression and continuity could be supported by a coherent set of thinking skills programmes from early years through to post-16, but this will only be achieved when teachers have the knowledge, skills and confidence to *infuse* thinking skills through all of their teaching.

Professor McGuinness defines infusion as 'to introduce into one thing a second thing which gives it extra life, vigour and a new significance.' Introducing a thinking skills approach into the primary and secondary school curriculum would have the aim of promoting metacognition by developing the following types of thinking:

- critical thinking
- decision-making
- creative thinking
- searching for meaning
- problem-solving.

A typical lesson in which thinking skills are infused would contain:

- an introduction which involved the pupils in discussing the aims and purpose of the learning
- challenging task(s)
- making explicit the kinds of thinking required
- appropriate questioning and dialogue
- pair/group work
- thinking about thinking
- making connections with other learning.

To achieve such a quiet revolution in learning and teaching, Professor McGuinness advocates 'powerful pedagogies' which can only be developed through collaborative CPD, with primary and secondary teachers sharing practice and reflection on that practice together. In this way, as primary and secondary schools become learning communities, progression and continuity become part of the way in which learning and teaching are carried out on a daily basis.

5–14, 5–13 or 5–12?

The paradox here is that while the 5–14 programme was designed to bring the primary and secondary curriculum together through a common structure, a common language and progressive levels of attainment, the two sectors remained stubbornly separate. Even when primaries were having to timetable curriculum areas in much the same way as secondaries had always done with subjects, there remained a view within secondary schools that somehow 5–14 was *easier* for primaries to implement. At worst, many secondary heads of department hoped that 5–14 might simply wither on the vine and become 5–12; at best, they believed that as the pressure increased on them to improve results at Higher, Standard Grade courses would begin in S3, the exams would take place in S3, leaving two full years for Highers, and, in passing, reduce 5–14 to 5–13.

If the curriculum is the context for learning, there is reason to be pessimistic that continuity and progression from P6 to S2 is any closer now than it was before 5–14 was introduced. On the other hand, many teachers in primary and secondary schools are now discussing learning and methodology rather than subject content and attainment levels in an effort to achieve continuity and progression. Learning styles, thinking skills, multiple intelligences, praise and rewards have all begun to feature in in-service training at the level of the school cluster, i.e. the secondary school, associated primaries and pre-five establishments. As we will see in Chapter 5, joint in-service training is becoming more common and may, in the longer term, be more successful in achieving continuity and progression than any national initiative.

SUMMARY

In recent decades, advances in our knowledge of the brain have opened up new possibilities for improving pupils' learning. Similarly, new theories of intelligence(s) have challenged traditional myths and, consequently, have called into question some of the long-standing practices within the education system such as setting, streaming, selection by 'ability' and even the age-and-stage nature of our schooling system. Theories of education have been re-visited and the role of the teacher re-considered, with new 'freedoms' being given by central government in recognition of the professional expertise of teachers. Thinking skills are now being considered as a way of focusing on the learning process and in so doing enabling teachers to achieve progression and continuity more successfully than in the past. Within the secondary school, thinking skills may offer a way of making learning more coherent across the curriculum. A collaborative approach, through CPD, may hold the key.

POINTS FOR REFLECTION

1 How much do teachers need to know about the new theories of learning, of the brain, of motivation, and the rest, to make their teaching more effective? What are the best ways of making such research accessible to teachers?

2 Can teachers and schools hake off the traditional views of intelligence which underpinned IQs, and are they prepared to re-assess their internal practices as a result?

3 Piaget and his view of *stages* of development have had a long and profound influence on Scottish education, particularly in the primary sector. Is it time for a re-assessment of these and other theories of learning?

4 How can we promote the similarities between primary and secondary schools rather than their differences?

5 Is the concept of the 10–14 teacher worth revisiting?

5 A question of aims?

> ❛ 'Oh Pooh!' said everybody else except Eeyore.
> 'Thank-you' growled Pooh.
> But Eeyore was saying to himself, 'This writing
> business. Pencils and what-not. Over-rated, if
> you ask me. Silly Stuff. Nothing in it.' ❜
>
> *Winnie the Pooh*, A. A. Milne

What is education for?

Why did Tony Blair famously argue that 'Education, Education,
Education' were the key political priorities for New Labour, and
why has he recently declared that (in England at least) we are
entering the 'post-comprehensive era'? What does society expect
from its schools, and as the twenty-first century unfolds, what
should schools be doing to prepare today's children for the
uncertainties and the challenges of tomorrow?

Schools are often seen as synonymous with education and yet
many have felt like Paul Simon in his song 'Kodachrome':

> When I think back on all the crap
> I learned in High school.
> It's a wonder I can think at all.

Others have felt like Eeyore did about writing; that much of what
schools did was a bit 'over-rated' and perhaps a little irrelevant.

There are four main arguments used when politicians argue
for education as a priority:

- economic
- social

- accountability
- human rights.

1. Economic

Tony Blair has argued that Great Britain has to retain its position in the world economy against competition from, for example, the 'tiger economies of the Pacific Rim'. A highly educated workforce is crucial and so we need to produce more young people with high levels of qualifications. Since national examinations are seen as the 'gold standard' in our education system, we need to encourage as many pupils as possible to achieve good exam passes. Therefore schooling in general is measured by exam success. Her Majesty's Inspectors have, over the past twenty years or so, placed huge emphasis on examination performance. The Conservative Government introduced 'league tables' in the 1980s, and in Scotland an audit unit was established within the inspectorate to focus attention on exam results. It developed a range of performance indicators which encompassed all aspect of school life, but it was examination statistics which dominated. Every year, the aggregated results of every pupil in S4, S5 and S6 were published by HMI in a form which could easily be converted into league tables. So, all newspapers, including the education journals, did just that, and the pupils, parents and staff of every secondary school in the country could see whether their school was top or bottom (or somewhere in between) of the league table for their local authority, or for Scotland as a whole. This process was justified on the grounds that standards needed to rise and that publication of results was a good thing, *pour encourager les autres*!

The economic argument, therefore, places huge emphasis on examination success. The aim of schools is to improve the performance, above all, of the more able pupils since they are the ones who will go on to generate economic success. However, this argument is problematic on a number of counts, not least that the relationship between school performance and economic success is highly complex. Not only that, since examinations rarely test the skills which business leaders claim we need in the workforce in the twenty-first century (creativity, problem-solving, team-work, adaptability, etc.), it is difficult to see how the number of Highers you have is predictive of the contribution you will make to the nation's economy. Nevertheless, this economic argument remains powerful, and the importance of tests and examinations as a measure of the success of schools has now reached the primary sector too.

2. Social

Some would argue that the biggest problem facing the world and this society is social inequality and exclusion. At a global level, the growing gap between the developed and the developing countries is a cause for concern and may help explain the rise of terrorism and fundamentalism in recent years. The growing gap between rich and poor is also a national phenomenon in Scotland and in the United Kingdom. Sociologists have coined the phrase 'the underclass' to describe a small but significant number of people who live below the poverty line, who have become detached and disenfranchised and who engage in anti-social behaviour. Thus, while there has been an overall rise in living standards, this underclass has become more entrenched.

In school terms, Michael Barber has written in his report *Young People and their Attitudes to School* (1994) of the 'disadvantaged, the disaffected and the disappeared'. This group of young people, most often from backgrounds which are impoverished in a range of ways, underachieve academically, cause disruption because of their anti-social behaviour and eventually simply absent themselves from the system, either by playing truant or by being excluded from school.

This analysis leads to a different emphasis from the economic argument. Instead of simply pushing the more able to do better and better in exams, we need to aim to achieve social cohesion and raise achievement for all. Thus, initiatives such as Early Intervention, introduced by the Scottish Executive in 1997, are geared towards raising general levels of achievement in the early years of education, but have the specific aim of closing the gap in achievement between the advantaged and the disadvantaged pupils. For many, this is problematic, since they see it as social engineering and fear that if will result in mediocrity. Indeed, the arguments against such interventions are not unlike those of the 1960s *Black Papers*, a series of polemical tracts which accused the comprehensive schools movement of promoting mediocrity and spurning excellence. Professor Bantock's famous dictum that 'the rise of the merely clever is a culturally doubtful manifestation' sums up their position succinctly. Evidence from the Early Intervention projects which have been underway longest would suggest that levels of attainment are indeed being raised, but that the gap, in some cases, is actually widening. The children of more advantaged backgrounds are taking most advantage of the new approaches! The aim of closing the gap is still difficult to achieve but for many it remains the key challenge of the twenty-first century.

3. Accountability

In the last 25 years or so, schools have been accused of being part of the problem, as well as part of the solution. The emphasis on accountability has been strong during that period, and remains so today. In England and Wales, the establishment of Ofsted heralded an agenda of 'failing' schools, which, unless they improved, would go to the wall in favour of 'good' schools. Competition was the spur to success, and public humiliation was the price of failure. This argument has much in common with the economic, since it judges success in terms of academic achievement as seen through examination results. 'If you can't measure it, it doesn't exist' would be the mantra of the proponents of this view.

They would have little sympathy for the social argument. Indeed, they would argue that schools have been hiding behind poverty as an excuse for their own underachievement. Thus if schools are the problem, then schools must find the solutions. To ensure that they do so, they must be inspected regularly, must use performance indicators developed by the Government's advisers, should undertake regular audits of their practice and should be compared publicly with other schools to ensure that they are performing as expected. Trust, autonomy and self-evaluation are paid lip-service by governments in this scenario and the bureaucracy which surrounds accountability impacts negatively on the morale of teachers. The locus of decision-making is outside of the school (and even of the local authority in England and Wales) and teachers do not feel 'empowered'.

4. Human Rights

In recent years, since the United Nations Declaration on Human Rights enshrined the principle that every child has an equal right to fulfil her/his educational potential, the so-called 'rights agenda' has had a high profile in education. Every child is born with the potential to be a successful learner; therefore if there are barriers of any kind we must seek to remove them. These barriers may be those which we have already discussed, namely, poverty and disadvantage, but may also include lack of care and love, disease, disability, prejudice, lack of opportunity and so on. Irrespective of the barrier, the duty rests with the education system to work with others if necessary to remove these barriers.

In Scotland, the rights of the child have been enshrined in legislation through the Children (Scotland) Act of 1995 and more recently the Raising Achievement in Scottish Schools Act of 2000. And in 2003, the Additional Support Needs legislation focused on the most vulnerable young people.

For many educationalists, the rights agenda is a direct descendant, philosophically, of the comprehensive school movement, the ideal of which was equality of opportunity. When Strathclyde Regional Council launched its report *Every Child is Special* in the early 1990s, it was an aspirational document rather than a description of the *status quo*. The problem, however, with the rights agenda, is that some people feel that a certain group of pupils is more special than other groups, and argue that emphasis on the most vulnerable is at the expense of the 'average' pupil. Since 1997 in Scotland, the most controversial educational initiative has been Inclusion, and the opposition from teachers is often predicated on the belief that many young people cannot be accommodated in mainstream schools, and that they, the teachers, cannot be expected to raise levels of achievement at the same time as tackling social exclusion. Quite simply, they see these two imperatives as mutually exclusive.

If we are to solve the problem of primary–secondary transition, we may need to ask whether the system that we have at present is actually working. But how would we know the answer if we are not clear about the aims of education in the first place, and the contribution that primary and secondary schools can make in achieving those aims?

A question of aims

Often when I do in-service training with teachers, particularly the staff of a school or cluster of schools, I ask them at some point to take a piece of paper and write down their school aims, *verbatim*.

Depending on the atmosphere in the room or hall, I will occasionally pretend that I will take in their efforts and mark them, just as teachers do with pupils' work. But, by this time they know I'm only joking, and since very few of them have actually begun to attempt the task, I confess that I am not serious. My point is, of course, that no one knows the school aims because they are often slightly pious, very general, probably aspirational and largely irrelevant! The only way to make aims relevant is to arrive at them through widespread and meaningful consultation, with all staff, pupils and parents. Not only that, they need to be revisited on a regular basis. And, above all, they need to be evaluated using a mixture of quantitative and qualitative evidence. 'Have we achieved our aims?' should be the key question asked at the end of each school year in every school in Scotland.

However, if schools are expected to have aims – and HMIE would be very disappointed if they were to arrive at a school which had no stated aims – then it is legitimate for schools to expect that the policy-makers have a clear set of aims for the whole education system.

Before looking at the Scottish education system, it might be worth considering the issue of aims from a global perspective. UNESCO has devised a set of aims for the twenty-first century:

- learning to know
- learning to do
- learning to live together
- learning to be.

The first and perhaps most obvious comment to a make is that 'learning' is at the heart of UNESCO's vision for education. Put in slightly different terms, learning is the 'core business' of education. However, the order of the UNESCO aims is interesting. It could be argued that the order simply reflects the importance placed on the various types of learning promoted by schools in most advanced industrial nations.

Learning to know

This is always the most highly valued aspect of education because knowledge transmission has been the traditional function of schools. Teachers teach and pupils passively learn, with a view to demonstrating their learning at some future point in an examination, probably of the paper-and-pencil variety. As mentioned above, in recent years, schools have been measured by the success of their pupils in these exams, and league tables have been published of schools in the press in much the same way as happens with football teams. Examinations have truly become 'high stakes' and target-setting regimes have been put in place to encourage schools to raise the levels of attainment of their pupils. Universities and the world of business and commerce continue to use examination passes as entry qualifications or sifting devices, even when, at the same time, they are claiming that they need young people who are flexible, adaptable, problem-solvers, team-workers and creative. Thus, if all of the emphasis is on exam results, it is hardly surprising that 'learning to know' is at the top of the list.

Learning to do

This aspect implies practical application of knowledge gained and the development of skills. Yet, it is still the case that so-called practical subjects in the Scottish curriculum still struggle to be valued equally with the traditional academic subjects. Subjects like technology, home economics, art, music and PE are afforded less time in the curriculum than maths or English, given less weight by university entrance officers and often seen as peripheral by pupils and parents. At an Ethos Network conference in 2003, the present author asked 150 S2 pupils from across Scotland what were the most important subjects in the school curriculum. The first answer was 'English' and the second, 'maths'. The next question was what were the least important subjects. The answers were 'RE', 'art', 'music' and 'home economics'. The final question was 'How do you come to those conclusions about what is important and what isn't?' The answer was pertinent, to the point and in some ways, from the pupils' perspective, a statement of the obvious; 'It's the amount of time which each subject gets. That's what tells you how important they are!' Out of the mouths of babes...

If a high-achieving pupil were to choose to do five Highers in S5 – art, music, home economics, graphic design and PE – how would the school react? Quite, simply, it would not be allowed to happen. In the primary school, things are not so very different. As we saw in Chapter 2, the balance of the primary curriculum is such that the practical subjects are grouped together under expressive arts or environmental studies which, *combined*, receive less time than English and maths together. And yet, in a real sense, we can only really claim to be educated when we can apply the knowledge and skills we acquire in school. The motto of the University of Strathclyde is *A place of useful learning*, but in schools, the usefulness takes second place to the knowledge itself. Learning to do simply does not have equal status to learning to know.

Learning to live together

In the twenty-first century, with the rise in terrorism, global tensions and bloody conflict in the name of religion or territorial advantage, it could be argued that *'learning to live together'* must be high on the agenda as a goal of worldwide education. Here in Scotland, we can claim to have made huge strides in this aspect of learning. In the early 1990s, the SOEID published a set of 'ethos indicators' for both primary and secondary schools. The idea was that schools could use the instruments, such as surveys, questionnaires, discussion topics, with staff pupils and parents to ascertain how each of these stakeholders perceived the school's value system. As a consequence of this interest in ethos, there was established a Scottish Ethos Network, based in Edinburgh University. It acted as a focal point for all the work being done on ethos across the country. It showcased the good work going on in schools up and down the country on anti-bullying initiatives, circle time, citizenship, the environment, peer counselling and peer support. Learning to live together, while not a formal part of the school curriculum, was a key aspect of effective schools, as Rutter and his colleagues had found in 1979.

In 2000, HMI published a report on the inspection of primary schools, entitled *'Educating the Whole Child'*. It looked at learning and teaching, links with the community and ethos, and found that 95 per cent of the schools inspected were either good or very good. Ethos had become a central part of school life. Two of the most positive inspectorate reports of the early 2000s, one on a secondary school in Stirling, the other on an infant school in East Lothian, found that each of the schools had an ethos which was very positive. Indeed, the phrase of which the headteacher of an East Lothian infant school was most proud was that the school had an 'ethos of giving'. This comment was due in no small part to the fact that the school was helping to raise funds to finance the building of a school in a favela in Brazil! Thus, while ethos and living together feature strongly among the criteria for school effectiveness, they still struggle to achieve equal status with the activities geared towards examination success.

Learning to be

This is an aim which might, at first glance, seem puzzling. And yet, when we look at it carefully, we can see elements of PSD, of religious and moral education and even of Daniel Goleman's theory of emotional intelligence. Here the idea is that education should help all young people discover who they are, why they are here, what is the nature is of their relationship with others, with the planet and with the values which bind societies together. Thus, spirituality, philosophy, development education and even evolution in its widest sense, may fall into this category of aim.

In many ways, the ideas which have been developed in recent years about intelligences, about the human brain, about learning styles and about motivation, fall into this category too. Before we can learn successfully we need to know about how we learn, how our brain works, what factors cause us to find some learning difficult and how we can develop metacognition.

These four UNESO aims seem relatively straightforward and unproblematic. However, I would argue that the order in which they are listed simply serves to reinforce the *status quo* as perceived by most advanced industrial nations. Learning to know is, of course, the most important because it can be measured by examinations which themselves act as a proxy for intelligence, and are the gateways through which privilege is accessed. The other three are simply 'also-rans'. It could be argued that the order should be reversed. Learning to be should be a fundamental of any modern educational system in the twenty-first century so that all young people can grow as individuals and fulfil their potential. Learning to live together post 9/11, could hardly be more important for the future of the planet. Learning to do is what most people think we need in the twenty-first century – problem-solving, creativity, teamwork and applied learning. Learning to know may be the least important of all in this age where the half-life of new knowledge is ever decreasing. What we need to be able to do is to find what we need to know, rather than to try to pack our brains full of facts and figures.

It is worth noting that in the first decade of the twenty-first century, many advanced industrial countries, successful and less successful, are re-visiting the aims of their educational system. From Tasmania to Norway, from Singapore to Scotland, there are national initiatives to re-define the fundamental principles of the formal (and informal) education system. In 2003, the Education Minister set up a review group to consider the principles of the curriculum 3–18 in Scottish schools. This is the first time since 1945 that such an attempt has been made to look at the curriculum in its entirety, rather than in stages. As part of the briefing for the group, a trawl was undertaken of the existing sets of aims and/or principles which underpin the Scottish curriculum; and there were quite a few!

The Scottish system

1 The national priorities

There are five national priorities for Scottish education as devised by the Scottish Executive in 2000:

1 **Achievement and attainment:** to raise standards of educational attainment for all in schools, especially, in the core skills of literacy and numeracy, and to achieve better levels in national measures of achievement including examination results.
2 **Framework for learning:** to support and develop the skills of teachers, the self-discipline of pupils and to enhance school environments so that they are conducive to teaching and learning.
3 **Inclusion and equality:** to promote equality and help every pupil benefit from education, with particular regard paid to pupils with disabilities and special educational needs, and to Gaelic and other lesser-used languages.
4 **Values and citizenship:** to work with parents to teach pupils respect for themselves and for one another, and their interdependence with other members of their neighbourhood and society, and to teach them the duties and responsibilities of citizenship in a democratic society.
5 **Learning for life:** to equip pupils with the foundation skills, attitudes and expectations necessary to prosper in a changing society and to encourage creativity and ambition.

These could be said to be *aims* or *aspirations* for the system as a whole. There is a hard edge to them in that the Scottish Executive expects schools and local authorities to plan within this framework and 'the Executive will monitor progress against those plans.' (*Educating for Excellence*, 2003).

2 Pre-school

According to SEED, a pre-school educational experience should produce 'confident, eager and enthusiastic learners' and pre-school education should aim to:

- provide a safe and stimulating environment in which children can feel happy and secure
- encourage the emotional, social, physical, creative and intellectual development of children
- promote the welfare of children
- encourage positive attitudes to self and others, and develop confidence and self-esteem
- create opportunities for play
- encourage children to explore, appreciate and respect their environment
- provide opportunities to stimulate interest and imagination;
- extend children's abilities to communicate ideas and feeling in a variety of ways.

The language here is more akin to the aims which individual schools might have and are very child-centred, as would be expected in the pre-five sector.

3 The 5–14 programme

The 5–14 programme has a set of principles (breadth, balance, continuity, coherence and progression) and it sets out the 'structured continuum of learning for all pupils to acquire and develop. The closest it comes to aims is the claim that the 5-14 curriculum should help pupils to be:

- confident, motivated and well-rounded
- literate and numerate
- fully understanding and able to play their part as citizens of a modern democratic society
- able to seize opportunities open to them, regardless of their background

- equipped with the skills and aptitudes to work flexibly and to embrace change throughout their lives.

4 The secondary curriculum

The secondary Guidelines document argues that the curriculum should provide experiences which will help young people to:

- live successful lives both now and in the future
- participate as active and responsible citizens
- cope with the changing world of work and the flexible labour markets of the future
- be highly motivated
- be confident and articulate
- value achievement and co-operation
- have high aspirations for themselves and their community
- think through major issues to form opinions and to work out values on which they will base their lifestyles
- have a commitment to learning
- have respect and care for self
- have respect and care for others have a sense of social responsibility.

Thus, the challenge is to ask, out all these fine-sounding words, what are the core aims of the education system, and are the aims across the sectors consistent? One way of doing this would be to look at the lists themselves to see if there are any common elements. In the context of 10–14, it is particularly important to ask if the 5–14 aims link in any way with what has gone before in early years education and what comes later from S3 onwards. Such a review of the aims which are currently used would suggest that, while the language differs a little from sector to sector, the following elements are common and add up to the following set of aims for the Scottish curriculum. It should promote:

- confidence
- well-rounded individuals
- citizenship
- creativity
- communication skills
- flexibility.

While each of these aims would need to be developed and examples given of how they might be achieved, they nevertheless provide a touchstone for the way in which the education system, especially at transition points, ensures that the needs of all pupils are met.

SUMMARY

Education has come to be seen by politicians as a priority in policy terms. There are several perspectives which are taken – economic, social, accountability and human rights – each of which can lead to different courses of action. A legitimate starting point for anyone wishing to improve education would be the clarification of aims, and UNESCO has offered four; learning to know, learning to do, learning to live together and learning to be. Scotland has five national priorities for education, and within the various initiatives from early intervention to national qualifications, there are sub-sets of aims. In addition to these, there are specific initiatives such as Assessment is for Learning, which have their own key aims and principles. The challenge for Scotland is to reach agreement among all those with a stake in education on what the aims should be in the twenty-first century.

POINTS FOR REFLECTION

1 Which of the four imperatives – economic, social, accountability and human rights – do you think has the most influence on educational policy-making in Scotland? Which of the four is most important to you?

2 Do you know your school's aims? Do you think they perform a useful function at present? What do you think of the UNESCO aims?

3 Are the national priorities helpful? If so, in what ways? If not, why not?

6 What does research tell us?

> Oh, here he comes, Piglet - with Rabbit.'
> 'Pooh,' asked Piglet, 'did you remember to help Owl remove that...'
> 'Of course, ' said Pooh. ' I have a phonographic memory, you know.'
> 'You mean,' said Rabbit, ' a photographic memory.'
> 'No,' insisted Pooh. 'Phonographic. It goes around and around. Sometimes it gets stuck. That's why I remember things so well.'
>
> **Winnie the Pooh, A. A. Milne**

Research, drunks and lampposts

A TES journalist suggested that 'politicians use research in much the same way as drunks use lampposts; more for support than illumination.' But it is not only politicians who have an ambivalent attitude to educational research. Nobody in schools trusts it either. While doctors read *The Lancet* to keep up with the latest medical research, teachers tend to read the Times Educational Supplement Scotland for the jobs, or maybe for the diaries of Morris Simpson. The TESS has a circulation of around 9,000 copies weekly, around one-sixth of the teaching profession. Albeit that many more teachers may read it in the staffroom for free, the penetration into the potential market is modest. So why have teachers traditionally eschewed research, and why have they been reluctant to engage with ideas, theory and issues surrounding policy-making?

The answer may lie in the inconclusive nature of some educational research. In 2002, the then Minister for Education, Sam Galbraith – a brain surgeon by training – lambasted educational research. He felt that it was woolly, unfocused and unreliable. He argued for a medical model, with control groups, double blind trials, control groups and, no doubt, placebos. What he did not realise was that there are ethical issues governing educational research which prevent children from being used as guinea pigs. He simply missed the point about educational research.

Educational research has a proud history in Scotland. The Scottish Council for Research in Education, until Mr Galbraith's intervention, was highly regarded, nationally and internationally. It had been established in the early twentieth century with financial support from the Scottish Education Department and the Educational Institute of Scotland (EIS), the major teaching union, and had served the educational community well over a number of years. The universities had also contributed to the research culture through their faculties of education, many of which had been former colleges of education, engaged in the training of teachers.

However, the key question is whether educational research has contributed substantially to the practice in schools. One way of attempting to answer this question is by taking a number of important issues and posing the question, 'what is the nature or the research evidence and how does it relate to day-to-day practice in schools?' The issues chosen are all relevant to the transition process between primary and secondary school, namely, class size, setting by prior attainment, and the transition process itself.

Class size

Class size is the issue which attracts the greatest level of support among professionals and parents. It is quite simple; everyone agrees that a reduction in class size would result in higher attainment among pupils. The problem is that there has been little in the way of hard evidence to support this commonsense view. When studies have been undertaken into the factors which affect pupil attainment, it has proved almost impossible to isolate the key variables which determine success or otherwise. When the quality of teaching, the composition of the class, socio-economic status, teaching methods and other variables are considered, it is well nigh impossible to identify class size as the key variable. The best teachers can, apparently, achieve success with large classes, while smaller classes do not always guarantee success. Chris

Woodhead, formally head of Ofsted, famously said that 'good teachers' could achieve good results from classes of 40-plus, a claim repeated on the television programme *Breakfast with Frost* by the then Education Secretary, David Blunkett.

The most definitive piece of research into class size and its effect on pupil attainment was the STAR Project which looked the immediate and long-term impact on pupil attainment on pupils in Texas schools. It found that when class size was reduced *significantly*, pupils made gains which lasted over time.

Professor Mary Simpson of Edinburgh University has reviewed the literature on class size and has concluded that any reduction has to be substantial if gains in attainment are to be made. By substantial she means that a class of 30-33, the norm for classes from P1 to S2 in Scottish schools, would have to be cut by half, to around 17. Her conclusion is that while smaller reductions might help ease teacher workload, there is no evidence that pupil attainment will rise. Perhaps the most important of Simpson's findings is that any reduction in class size must be accompanied by changed in methodology, if significant gains are to be made.

In 2003, as a result of the National Debate in Scotland, SEED produced a document entitled *Educating for Excellence*. It summarised nine key priorities 'to meet children's individual needs'. Not all of them were based on research evidence. Indeed, some of them illustrate the way in which education policy operates like a pendulum, swinging quite dramatically at times, more gradually at others. The issue of pupil choice is a good case in point. At the beginning of the 1970s, the amount of pupil choice in the secondary school was considerable: English and maths were the only core subjects. By the 1980s, the core included eight modes, including creative and aesthetic subjects, technology and social subjects; pupils' choice was limited. In the primary school, teacher choice was a key feature until the late 1980s when the 5–14 programme created what some have called 'Scotland's National Curriculum', and all pupils had to spend the same amount of time each week on English language, maths, expressive arts, environmental studies, PSD and religious and moral education.

Key Priorities

Increase pupil choice by reviewing the school curriculum to suit twenty-first century needs and to reduce substantially the current overload in the 5–14 curriculum. We will establish which subjects might form a well-balanced core around which pupils will have expanded access to choices such as vocational training.

Simplify and reduce the amount of assessment to cut down the number of tests and exams and the amount of time spent on them. We have started this work, but we will look at more radical options such as only sitting exams when pupils leave school instead of every year from S4.

Bring forward proposals to reduce class sizes and improve pupil/teacher ratios at critical stages such as P7, S1 and S2, particularly in maths and English, and have more learning in small groups. We must make sure that pupils will benefit from falling school rolls over the next decade.

Tackle discipline problems and bullying by fully implementing the recommendations of the Discipline Task group, reviewing their impact and taking further action where necessary.

Improve school buildings to create a school estate in which all of the schools have the right facilities, are well designed, well built and provide a flexible environment which continues to meet future needs.

Give more control over budgets to headteachers so that the people closest to the children can decide how best to use resources. Introduce greater flexibility for schools and education authorities through local agreements for excellence.

Have teachers work across primary and secondary schools. We will act to make sure that this flexibility is being used to deliver the best education for pupils and help them make the transition from primary to secondary.

Involve parents more in their children's education by providing new national guidelines giving parents access and by reviewing and reforming the role of School Boards and Parent Teacher Associations.

Strengthen the role of inspection by delivering clearer and more frequent reports to parents and focusing more directly on schools which need to improve. Consider what additional powers may be required to ensure underperformance is tackled.

(*Educating for Excellence*, 2003)

On the issue of class size, although the research evidence of its benefits has existed for some time, it is only now that the political will has emerged to make a change.

Setting, streaming and mixed ability

One of the most contentious issues in education revolves around how pupils should be grouped or organised into classes. Traditionally, primary classes were 'mixed ability', in other words, all pupils at a certain stage, irrespective of ability, were in the same class and the teacher tailored the work to the different abilities of the pupils. In secondary schools, this was not the norm. Until the mid-1960s, pupils were selected by a Qualifying Examination for either a junior secondary (vocational) school or a senior secondary (academic) school. On arrival, they were streamed, i.e., put into classes by some measure of general ability, and they went to every subject as a class, irrespective of specific aptitudes. When comprehensive education was introduced in the 1960s, streaming disappeared, and pupils were in mixed ability classes for the first two years, and were then set (not streamed) by ability in specific subjects. Thus a pupil could be in the top set for some subjects, the second set for others, and so on. As time went on, setting began to be introduced into S2, and by the mid-1990s, HMI were recommending it for some subjects as early as S1. By the 2000s, it had begun to appear in the upper stages of primary.

So, what is the research evidence on the relative merits of mixed ability and setting? As indicated in Chapter 1, the most comprehensive review on the subject ever undertaken in Scotland was conducted by the Scottish Council for Research in Education (SCRE). It was commissioned by HMI to inform their review of practice in S1 and S2. But, when the report was published as *Achievement for All* in 1996, there was no reference to the SCRE survey. The HMI report recommended that schools make more extensive use of setting in S1 and S2 in order to raise attainment. However, when the SCRE report was finally published in 1997 under the title *Setting and Streaming*, strangely enough, it did not conclude that setting did actually raise attainment. Instead it suggested that the research to date was inconclusive! While it was possible to find some studies that supported the view that the most able pupils in maths did slightly better in sets, others concluded that the least able did less well. Overall, there was no overwhelming evidence one way or the other. However, there were a number of studies which suggested that in lowest sets it was likely that teachers underestimated the potential of pupils, that pupils in these low sets had lower expectations than similar pupils who were in mixed ability classes and that movement from one set to another was limited.

However, it was the research by Dylan William and his colleagues at Kings College London which challenged the most deep-seated assumptions of the teaching profession. The researchers interviewed pupils who were in top maths sets in secondary schools. They found that a significant number of pupils reported that they felt under pressure by virtue of being in the top set. Teachers constantly referred to forthcoming exams and to their expectations that all pupils in the top set would get the highest grades. In addition, the pupils felt that the subject itself was now less interesting than before. Teaching methods had narrowed and there was now much more didactic, whole-class teaching and fewer opportunities for group work or more 'fun' methods. Most surprisingly of all, perhaps, was the finding that some pupils had feelings of guilt. They believed that there were other pupils who could, and perhaps should have been in the top sets too. In short, being in the top set was not regarded by these pupils as the unalloyed privilege that most teachers would have predicted.

More recent studies into setting and mixed ability (Smith and Sutherland, 2002; 2003) have indicated that there are problems associated with setting which are often underplayed in the advice given to schools by HMIE and politicians. The current writer was asked in 2003 by a Council in Scotland to assist in coming to a decision about a request from six secondary schools to depart from the existing policy on mixed ability classes in S1 and S2. The main reasons advanced by the schools was the pressure from senior management to meet 5–14 targets set nationally for the percentage of pupils who should achieve Level F by the end of S2. This, coupled with concerns about the workload imposed on staff by having all levels of attainment in one class, and concerns about the 'pace of learning' of learning of S1 and S2 classes expressed by HMIE, caused these schools to seek permission to set in S2 or before. As one principal teacher of English said, 'Mixed ability is just too difficult. It's too difficult for me and it's too difficult for my staff.' Indeed, it transpired that some of the schools had already move towards setting in S2 for these very reasons.

A decision was taken to invite the researcher to each of the schools to observe classes, mixed ability and set, to talk to staff and pupils, and to look at evidence which the schools had gathered to support their claims that setting was more effective. The visits took place and the picture which emerged was a complex one. All of the schools had mixed ability classes in S1. All of the staff consulted were happy with this and indeed there was often a strong relationship forged between the teacher and the class. Support was usually available for pupils with additional support needs, and the class teachers were fairly confident that pupils' needs were being met. Many staff referred back to the days when they used to take their S1 class on to S2, and were unhappy that they no longer did so. In the schools which had already set in S2, the staff and pupils in the top sets seemed happy with the arrangement. Pupils spoke of the absence of disruption from unmotivated peers, of the atmosphere in the class of not being teased for being bright. Some of them felt that the pace was now too fast and that some of their friends could and should have been in the top set too. Some had concerns about the effect on these friends of not being in the top set.

The picture which emerged in the other sets which were 'broad-banded' was quite different. In these classes, the teachers were not happy, in the main. They had lost the top six or seven pupils from their mixed ability S1 class and had taken in six or seven others so that the class sizes were roughly equal. The effect of this was to create classes where motivation was lower, where low-level indiscipline was higher and where the ethos was less positive. In other words, the creation of the top (or Level F) class seemed only to benefit a minority of pupils. One school, which had resisted the pressure to set, had produced evidence that with appropriate methods, pupils at all levels were improving in the mixed ability classes. One other school, in the course of the discussions, reverted to mixed ability in S2. The others remained convinced that setting was better.

This is a good illustration of the ambivalence of teachers towards research. They want policy to be based on research, but are sometimes happy to reject research evidence when it does not support their views or runs counter to other pressures. As for research itself, it is rarely conclusive and often serves to highlight issues rather than provide answers in all circumstances.

Primary–secondary transition

Research into the effects of primary–secondary transition on pupils is not extensive in the UK. The 10–14 report reviews the extant research for its 1986 report and since then there have been few studies undertaken on the issue. In 2000, Boyd and Simpson were commissioned by Angus Council to conduct research into S1 and S2. This involved visits to primary schools to interview pupils and staff at the P7 stage, only weeks before the move to secondary school. The pupils were tracked as they moved into S1 and the researchers shadowed classes for days at a time, interviewed groups of pupils, teachers, senior managers and parents, studied school documentation and observed lessons. The result was a report, *Towards a framework for effective learning and teaching*:

Towards a framework of effective learning and teaching

- The quality of teaching in primary and secondary schools was high overall, but variable across secondary departments.
- Arrangements for the transition to secondary schools were thorough and supportive.
- Continuity of learning and teaching P7 to S1 was conspicuous by its absence.
- Coherence across the secondary curriculum was non-existent.
- Fragmentation was a feature of S1 and S2, with thirteen to fourteen teachers per class being the norm.
- Setting by attainment was on the increase in S2, and, in some cases in S1, though the rationale was problematic and the commitment to evaluation patchy.
- S2 and S1, in that order, were timetabled last in the secondary school, reflecting the importance PTs gave to this stage.
- The 'fresh start approach' in S1, criticised by HMI in 1993, was alive and well in most schools and in most departments.
- Pupils liked secondary school – the variety, the specialist subjects and the teachers – but reported a lack of challenge and a feeling that teachers did not know what they could achieve.

(Boyd and Simpson, 2000)

The research demonstrated that there was a range of practice across the schools and across departments within the same school. It uncovered a number of attitudes among secondary staff which were worrying.

The reliability of assessments carried out by primary staff as seen by their secondary counterparts also emerged as an issue. A conversation between a principal teacher, an assistant principal teacher of maths and the researcher, highlighted these issues. When asked how the maths classes were organised in S1, the APT stated that the classes were set from S1 onwards, using 5–14 levels. The reason given was that mixed ability classes were impossible to teach in maths. When the fact that primary classes are mixed ability was raised, the APT countered by saying that primary teachers did not really *teach* maths; they simply put work on the board and went round the class helping individuals. The PT was asked if he was happy with the assessment information he received form the primary school. He said that he was far from happy with it and felt that no two primary schools had the same view of 5–14 levels. Quite simply, the assessments could not be relied upon. When asked why, in that case, the classes were set in S1 using 5–14 levels, he responded by saying that 5–14 national test information was the best he had, and so he used it until October, and thereafter, relied upon the department's own assessment.

A role for research in education?

Millions of pounds are spent annually on educational research in Scotland, by the Scottish Executive, by universities, by local authorities or by other public and private funding bodies. Much of it is policy-led, arising out of the priorities set by government. There are large-scale collaborative projects and there are small-scale, single teacher action research initiatives. In total, at any one time, there is a lot of research activity going on. A key question must be, 'what impact does it have on practice in schools?'. The answer, however, is not clear cut. Probably, the best we can say is 'we don't know'. Unless teachers in schools are aware of the research going on, are able to access the findings, and have time to reflect on how it might impact on their practice, it is difficult to see how they would ever know if research was ever making a difference.

Identifying the role which research should play is not much easier. An SOED-funded project to examine the link between

research and staff development, *Of Drunks and Lampposts*
(1994), outlined a number of different purposes of research and
quoted from a range of people involved in education to illustrate
each one.

Of Drunks and Lampposts

Informing – proving insights which might influence policy and practice:
'There was a constant flow of research and school self-evaluation was being informed by it.'

Clarifying – playing a role in making issues easier to understand:
'Research doesn't give answers; it contributes ideas.'

Illuminating – providing an informed perspective and giving alternatives:
'All that research can do is to ask a series of questions and lay a series of alternatives from which people can choose in terms of policy or practice.'

Supporting – giving credence to and justification for approaches:
'It can be used to prop up Government policy, very often on a very selective basis. It can also be used, again selectively, to support the dominant ideology of the time.'

Sharing practice – pin-pointing good practice and sharing it with others:
'The long time-lag which research often has means that ideas are only taken up long after the initial research has been completed.'

Validating – confirming what we already believe to be effective:
'It would appear to the outsider that the research which is currently bring funded is simply an attempt to legitimise the process of 5–14.'

Challenging – putting ideas and practices under the microscope and hold them to account
'The whole notion of exploring ideas, of challenging assumptions, was something which the system had to contain.'

Underpinning policy – no policies should be made unless based on research.

Destabilising – shaking up the system
'Of course, the problem is that research can often give the answers which the funders do not want to hear.'

(pp. 13–15)

The issue of primary–secondary transition has not featured highly in the educational research priorities over the years. The Boyd-Simpson study (2000) was relatively small-scale. However the interest which its findings provoked suggests that more research in this area would be welcomed. Perhaps, too, there needs to be a more extensive debate on the models of educational research which might yield more credible results. Instead of the researcher doing research *on* teachers and pupils and schools, they should be doing it *with* them. In this way, a collaborative model might emerge where those who are the subject of the research feel some ownership of the process and feel a commitment to validity and reliability of the methods being used. Thus, the findings of the research may be more likely to influence policy and practice.

SUMMARY

While Scotland has a proud history of educational research embodied in SCRE, it remains true that politicians and teachers alike have been sceptical of its contribution to the improvement of the system. On contentious issues such as class size or setting by ability, the research evidence, though considerable, has rarely been conclusive enough to persuade doubters. Research into primary–secondary transition has fared little better even when evidence of the 'fresh start' approach seemed conclusive, notwithstanding more than a decade of the 5–14 programme. Perhaps what is needed is more debate on the role of educational research and a greater degree of partnership between researchers and teachers in schools.

POINTS FOR REFLECTION

1. What should be the role of educational research?

2. How would you go about trying to undertake research as a school or classroom level? What support would you need?

3. Which of the conclusions from the national debate do you feel would benefit from further research?

4. Why do teachers sometimes choose to ignore the findings of research?

7 Problems and opportunities: listening to young people their parents

> 'Hallo, Eeyore,' said Christopher Robin, as he opened the door and came out. 'how are you?'
> 'It's snowing still,' said Eeyore, gloomily.
> 'So it is.'
> 'And freezing.'
> 'Is it?'
> 'Yes,' said Eeyore. 'However,' he said, brightening up a little, 'we haven't had an earthquake lately.'
>
> *Winnie the Pooh*, A. A. Milne

Different perspectives

The transition from primary to secondary school is a rite of passage. It signals, at least for the parents of many of the 11- and 12-year-olds, a loss of innocence, a first step towards adolescence, a growing up. For these same parents, it can be a point where their active involvement in their child's education begins to tail off. They may feel that their level of expertise is no longer sufficient, and regard the secondary teachers as experts. They may, in some sense, simply hand over their offspring to the secondary school, confident that the staff know what they are doing. In short, they may begin to take a step back from the education process.

For the pupils, there are opportunities and there are fears. As we will see, many of them experience both emotions at the same time. The attractiveness of the 'big' school lies in its mystery, in its possibilities of doing grown-up things like going to the shops at lunchtime and in its complexity with all of the specialist departments and the hi-tech facilities. At the same time, they are concerned about being the smallest and youngest, about the prospect of bullying and arcane rituals of initiation, and they worry about the amount of work they may be asked to do.

That many of these fears are unfounded, and indeed the opposite of what is in fact facing them, is of little consequence. Essentially, these are matters of perspective. This is one powerful reason why we should, more often and more systematically than at present, give pupils and parents an opportunity to talk about their fears and aspirations. It may just be that they may give us insights which we would not otherwise get and they may be able to offer some solutions to the problems of transition.

In this chapter we will look at what pupils and parents say about transition, in Scotland and elsewhere in the United Kingdom. We will see what they say about the standard of work they are asked to do, about behaviour and bullying, about the characteristics of effective teachers and about guidance and pastoral care. We will also explore views on homework, punishments and rewards and the whole issue of the role of parents and pupils in decision-making in Scottish schools.

Going to the 'big school' – a UK perspective

In her chapter 'Going to "the big school": the turbulence of transition' (1996), Jean Rudduck, the pre-eminent chronicler of pupils' views in the United Kingdom, refers to the picture painted a decade earlier by Delamont and Galton of pupils' first days at secondary school. It is a poetic picture of fear and menace, of the secondary school as 'disaster's cavern' and the whole experience has a kind of sinister foreboding. However, Rudduck argues that by 1996, her own study shows that while there is some apprehension, there is also excitement and even 'eager anticipation'. She points out that by the time most pupils enter the secondary school at the beginning of S1, they have already visited the school, have read the booklet(s) which the secondary school has produced for them and may even have attended sports days or open evenings with or without their parents.

While general levels of anxiety seemed to have fallen in the decade between these two studies, there were still issues which worried pupils as they arrived in secondary:

> ...our old school... wasn't a small school but you still, like, in some ways, you knew their name and there was no, I mean, there

was no troubles, with not really people stealing anything. Just like some people took things out of lunch boxes, like a chocolate biscuit.

(p. 20)

Personal property, theft, nowhere to put bags and personal security generally were all things which these pupils raised. This can lead to a sense of awkwardness about the new place, how to react, how to behave, and even how to dress at the school disco:

We ended up wearing jeans and a nice top and we wore high heels. And everyone else was in like trainers and shell suits and I just felt so out of place.

(p. 21)

On a day-to-day basis, the biggest fear was of getting lost in the new building, of wandering about unable to find the classroom, unsure of whom to ask and fearful of being late. This was true of the present writer in 1960, and was true also of Rudduck' respondents in 1996:

I were in PE once and I never got there until about the end of the lesson. I couldn't find the way.

(p. 21)

The issue of rules emerged as a contributory factor to the confusion which could be felt by the new First Years. New ways of doing things, each, no doubt, with its own rationale, seemed complicated to the new pupils:

You can't take your coat or bag into the dining room at lunchtime – unless your sandwiches [and then] you can take your bag in [but] not your coat, so you have to leave your coat...'

(p. 21)

Silberman (1971) refers to the 'sheer complexity' of pupils' experiences when they arrive in secondary school. But Rudduck found that pupils also reported finding unexpected benefits in being in the new school. The move from having only one teacher for all or most of the week in primary school to having upwards of twelve or thirteen was seen as a positive move by some pupils:

If there's a teacher you don't like you're not stuck with them for every single lesson every day of the year.

(p. 22)

Other pupils were aware that variety might not outweigh the fragmentation caused by having too many teachers. The experience of one pupil might not have been entirely typical, but it was heartfelt:

[we] had, like, 32 different teachers because we had supply teachers and we even had the school secretary once.

(p. 23)

Few pupils ever go home and tell their parents about the number of supply teachers they have in any one day. It's a relatively hidden problem but a source of anxiety not just for the school staff who have to manage it, but also for some of the pupils.

A big plus for the pupils in Rudduck's study was the specialist facilities which secondary schools had to offer. They seemed to associate this with a 'better education'. However, absence from school was a worry and the associated problem of 'falling behind'. They worried, too, about bullying, from older pupils, and about name-calling from peers. They often spoke of peers who, for a variety of reasons, had started falling behind and were now not attending regularly. It was a kind of downward spiral.

Rudduck singles out homework as a specific issue. Some pupils see early on that this is important and settle into a pattern of doing it on time and to a high standard. They bring their homework diary every day and involve their parents in the process. Others see it as a chore and begin to find ways of avoiding its completion, seeing the punishment exercises which might result as a minor irritant, and keeping their parents out of the loop. If bad habits are established as early as the first two years of secondary, it bodes ill for the pupils' future prospects of school success.

For the majority of pupils, it was the challenge of new learning which was uppermost in their minds. Rudduck reports the 'enormous effort' which staff put into making S1 pupils feel at home. She refers to documentation, social-bonding events and inter-house competitions designed to heighten their sense of being part of a group. Meanwhile, some of the older pupils were providing a counter balance, reinforcing the new pupils' sense of being the youngest, the lowest in the pecking order. But, the biggest challenge of all is how to accommodate themselves to the 'different styles and personalities' of their new teachers.

Rudduck suggests five things which schools might do to help lay a 'good foundation' for pupils' experience of secondary school:

- Give more status to pupils, as early as S2.
- Create time for a 'dialogue about learning'.
- Start 'futures counselling' in small groups.
- Strengthen the procedures and practices relating to homework.
- Respond to the problem of 'catching up' for pupils who have missed work. (p 26)

She finishes her chapter with an observation:

We do not underestimate the difficulty of learning to be a pupil!

Transition in Scotland: have things moved on?

When a council in Scotland approached two experienced researchers and commissioned them to undertake a small-scale study into primary–secondary transition, the emphasis was on exploring the reasons for underachievement among pupils in the first two years of secondary school. The context for the study was the 1996 HMI report, *Achievement for All*, which as we saw in Chapter 1, expressed concerns about levels of achievement among S1 and S2 pupils and recommended that there should be timetabling arrangements made to reduce the number of teachers seen by S1 and S2 classes each week, more setting by attainment in the early years of secondary school and more direct teaching. The publication of *Achieving Success in S1 and S2*, sharpened the focus and suggested criteria which should be met if subjects were to be included in the S1 and S2 curriculum. It also changed direct teaching to 'direct interactive teaching' and defined it in a way which included a range of collaborative approaches and softened the line on setting, suggesting the kinds of questions schools should consider before embarking on such a strategy.

The reason for all of this attention on S1 an S2 was another round of AAP publications which suggested that for most pupils their rate of progress in S1 and S2 was not as high as might be expected by their achievements in the later stages of primary school. International studies such as TIMMS, the third international mathematic survey, suggested that Scottish pupils were not achieving as well as their counterparts in other countries. And, closer to home, government targets for achievement within the 5–14 programme were not being met.

Meanwhile, councils responsible for schooling were under pressure from HMI and from the Scottish Executive to be demonstrating 'Best Value' in their provision of services to their constituents. There were concerns that primary–secondary transition, and in particular, the structure of the S1 and S2 curriculum were part of the problem, and the commissioning to external researchers might provide some objective evidence on which the Council might base decisions about its course of action.

The Council wanted researchers to spend some time in four of the secondary schools and in some of their associated primary schools. The methodology was to be largely qualitative, interviewing pupils, teachers and parents; shadowing classes for a day at a time; reviewing school documentation; and looking at the issue of mixed ability versus setting, which was contentious in the authority. In the event, the findings were significant, not just in finding answers but in providing for the secondary schools a possible way forward in terms of discussing learning and teaching.

The views of the pupils were insightful, not least when it came to the business of learning and teaching itself:

Interviewer: So, what do you think makes the most difference to how well you do?

Pupil: I think it is mainly the teacher.

Interviewer: What specifically about the teacher?

Pupil: Him being able to take your problems and discuss the problems over with you and sort of help you understand more or less about them.

(p. 41)

The relationship with the teacher was the key issue for the pupils, more important than hard work and interest in the subject:

> I find that I can relate to the teacher in English better. I can just speak to him – he is a friend as well. I like to work hard so he knows it is my thanks to him. (p. 41)

This issue of working hard for the teacher has long been part of the Scottish education system. It could be argued that what we want to happen is that pupils want to work not just hard but successfully *for themselves*, not for the teacher. The goal of education, as McLean has argued (2003), should be *intrinsic* motivation, not *extrinsic*. The model of the 'good student' who is conformist, passive, works hard for the teacher, does as s/he is told, gives the teacher the answers s/he wants, may seem like every teacher's dream. However, it may not be developing in the learners the skills and attitudes they will need to become independent, creative, flexible and adaptable learners.

However, from the pupils' perspective, it was important that there be a good relationship between teacher and learners. It allowed the teacher to be more sensitive to the strengths and weaknesses of the pupils, and in turn, pupils were less inhibited about asking for help:

> If you're stuck, you can just go up to him and he will sit and go over it and he will say, 'Go home and do it, and come back, and we will see if it is right or not.
>
> (p. 41)

It is possible to argue that the key element in the teaching and learning process is not the relationship but the strategies which the teachers gives to the learners to help them tackle new problems or even familiar problems in new contexts. However the climate of the classroom is clearly important. In 1996, the 10–14 report suggested that 'the classroom crackles with subliminal signals.'

In 2000, the comment from an S1 pupil echoed these sentiments:

> You feel you are making an idiot out of yourself asking the teacher. She says [funny voice] 'If there's anybody out there who doesn't understand, put your hand up and I'll help you.' But everybody feels they are making an idiot out of themselves, so you don't bother.
>
> (p. 41)

These subliminal signals here are clearly negative and the pupil's response is to disengage. If the aim of the teacher is to promote *understanding*, then the next pupil's words may be a salutary warning:

I shouldn't think he'd notice if I didn't understand. But he'd notice
if I wasn't working.

(p. 41)

In mitigation, if the teacher is under pressure to 'get through the
curriculum', as many reported they were; if HMI are continually
emphasising 'pace of learning' without explaining what they
mean; and if 'better behaviour' is seen to be prior to 'better
learning" it is easy to understand why 'working' seems more
important than 'understanding'.

Feuerstein argues that the teacher is a mediator and that his job
is to give the learners the essential concepts and strategies to enable
them to learn. This 'learning how to learn' or 'metacognition' is at
the heart of the education process. Pupils, intuitively understand
this:

The teachers are all very helpful in all subjects, but if only they'd
just sit down with you and tell you how you're doing and things.
And if you're not good at something, tell you what you could do.

(p. 41)

Good relationships are necessary but not sufficient if learning is
the goal:

I know I'm not good at spelling. She just says, 'You'll need to
work on your spelling', but I don't know how.

(p. 41)

A recurring theme in discussions with S1 and S2 pupils is
'challenge', or, rather, the lack of it:

It was too slow in first and second year.

(p. 42)

Indeed, one pupil who had felt all along that she had been placed
in a group below her ability in maths on the basis of a pre-test
which she didn't understand, had developed a self-preservation
strategy:

Well, I just take my time. I don't hurry myself.

The conclusion from the interviews with S1 and S2 pupils was
that they liked secondary school, they liked the variety and they

liked the specialist subjects which had their own dedicated accommodation. However, they did not feel that they were being challenged and often were resentful about having to do things which they could already do, and had already done in P6.

Primary pupils' views on transition

As part of research into pupils' views of Guidance in the secondary school (Boyd and Lawson 2003), pupils in P5, P6 and P7 were asked about the kinds of issues on which they sometimes had to ask for advice. Among these was the transition to the secondary school.

P5 pupils listed among their concerns:

- scared of getting lost
- stories of being 'egged'
- excited about new subjects
- worried about losing friends/excited about making new ones.

It was a mixed picture. The move to secondary was more than two and a half years away and the levels of anxiety were relatively low.

P6 pupils raised some of the same issues:

- excited about the prospect of making new friends/scared about not being with current friends
- scared of being bullied by older pupils
- worried about hard work, older kids and the size of the school
- aware that they would now be the youngest in the school.

Interestingly, almost all of the P7 pupils were positive about going to the secondary. Almost all of them had met staff from the secondary, most commonly Guidance staff. They were about to visit the secondary too, and messages from friends and older siblings were largely positive. The concerns which did surface were not strongly felt and included being split up from friends, not being given responsibility and being bullied.

This study into pupils' perspectives on Guidance supported the evidence from previous studies in demonstrating the problem is not one of 'transition' *per se*. Staff in secondary and associated primary schools work very hard to smooth the transition for pupils, especially the most vulnerable. Visits, activities, open days and evenings as well as documentation, all help to de-mystify the secondary schools for P7 pupils. The problem is much more to do with curriculum structures, lack of progression continuity and progression, and teacher expectations.

Able pupils – a SNAP judgement?

The publication of the HMI report *The Education of Able Pupils, P6 to S2* in 1993, marked a minor turning point in Scottish education. Hitherto, it had been difficult to raise the issue of able pupils for fear of being labelled 'elitist'. The reasons for this are complex. The move away from selective schooling, the Qualifying Examination (Eleven Plus in England and Wales) and streaming pupils by general ability, had made the education system wary of labelling pupils. There were pressure groups including the National Association for Gifted Children (Scotland) which often focused on the failings of the state system and agitated for separate treatment for the gifted. Even the terminology was problematic, with 'gifted', 'able', 'more able', 'talented' and so on all having their adherents and all representing different perspectives on the issue. The HMI report was very balanced, rejecting simplistic solutions to the problems of meeting the needs of able pupils and distancing itself from any ideological positions on mixed-ability, setting, 'hot-housing' or acceleration through the curriculum. Instead, as noted in Chapter 6 above, the report stated **in bold**, that 'the fresh start approach in Secondary 1 is no longer tenable' and challenged schools to develop 'an ethos of achievement'.

In 1995, Dr Paquita McMichael and the present author conducted a small-scale research study in two local authorities in Scotland into schools, primary and secondary, which were recognised as having an ethos of achievement. In the resulting report, *Towards a Climate of Achievement* (1996), McMichael and Boyd included the views of pupils on a range of aspects of achievement, including the primary–secondary differences. Pupils in S1 and S2 reported feelings of underachievement, of doing things they had already done in the primary school. They talked of having to wait until others caught up and of being given tedious 'extension' work:

> Sometimes you could go further but they don't let you. You have to wait until the others catch up. You do workcards and stuff. Workcards are boring – just more of the same.

This is echoed by an S2 pupil who said that she 'never wanted to see another extension worksheet in her life!', while another offered some practical suggestions to her teachers: 'You could do art work, quiet reading, TV, writing and things instead.'

Indeed, the pupils were absolutely clear that they wanted to achieve as much as they could, and saw that a range of teaching methods was necessary, citing times when they liked working in groups and times when they wanted to work alone. Above all, they were adamant that the approaches to recognising achievement which most primary schools have in place were transferable to the secondary school: reward systems, well done boards and the use of critical friends in class, were all mentioned positively. The able pupils, often caricatured as being the butt of negative peer-group pressure, seemed willing to take it in their stride, and were happy to have their achievements recognised, albeit sensitively and appropriately.

Shortly after the publication of the HMI report, the Scottish Network for Able Pupils was set up. The title of the network was chosen carefully so that its acronym was an ironic comment on the prevailing metaphor for meeting the needs of able pupil. It seemed that most people felt that able pupils had to be 'stretched' and this had connotations of accelerating learning, pushing them further and faster to learn more and to sit exams earlier. The Networks Advisory Committee was wary of such simplistic representations of what it felt to be a complex issue, and so SNAP was to serve as a reminder of what can happen if something or someone is stretched too far. SNAP is still going strong and continues to work with schools, local authorities and parents to help them to promote an ethos of achievement (contact SNAP@educ.gla.ac.uk and see www.ablepupils.com).

Parents' perspectives

It has to be said that parents' views of Scottish schools are generally very positive. One only has to look at the evidence from HMIE parent questionnaires, the data from the National Debate and the findings from a range of research studies. Occasionally, this implicit support for schools rises to the surface, usually in times of crisis. When Strathclyde Regional Council attempted in the mid 1980s to close schools as part of its *Adapting to Change* strategy, the one thing which was entirely predictable was that as soon as a school's name appeared on the hit-list for closure, it took barely 24 hours for a Parents' Action Group to spring up, a march to take place to the council headquarters and a campaign to fight the closure to be planned. It did not seem to matter whether the school was in a leafy suburb or in an area of social disadvantage. It was clear that the vast majority of parents in Scotland support their local school.

In their study on S1 and S2 (2000), Boyd and Simpson sought the views of parents. They found that 'in the main, parents were happy with the quality of the experiences' their children were receiving. Their main concerns at the point of transfer to the secondary school echoed those of the pupils in the Guidance study (above), including separation from friends. In addition, some were concerned about behaviour on buses and the dearth of information about clubs and other extra-curricular activities.

Communications with the school was a big issue for parents:

> [A good school is one which ...] keeps in contact with the parents, keeps parents informed. Our secondary seems to; there is a lot of communication, about learning and the curriculum. (p. 42)

An issue which emerged for many parents was work home, as opposed to homework:

> We'd asked him to get books home for maths we wanted to check up – but they don't seem to do that. Unless you ask you don't get. We both have maths and I like to be involved and know what's expected, but I don't know the syllabus.

Parents were very clear that the ethos of the school was of paramount importance:

> I like to think a good school is somewhere where each child is valued; where their strengths and weaknesses are seen and they are encouraged ... Where teachers are kind to the children.

Indeed, parents' views of the long-term effects of schooling are far more realistic and well-rounded than those of many of the politicians whom they elect:

> The most important thing is his happiness, and what he feels comfortable with. He is bright. He should do well and go on to HE.

The evidence from the national debate supports the views of these parents. In general, parents are happy with the comprehensive system in Scotland, but they are concerned about underachievement in the early stages of secondary school. They do not always feel that the secondary school is easy to understand or is as accessible as the primary had been. They trust the staff to do their best for the pupils, but they are not convinced that parents' views, knowledge of their children or ability to help with learning are taken into account. In general, as they see it, there is room for improvement. Finally, the views of parents, while in the main supportive of the system, can also offer valuable insights into the effect of policies on them and on their children.

SUMMARY

Since the 1980s, the views of pupils and parents on many aspects of education have begun to form an important part of the research evidence. At a UK level, Rudduck has chronicled the views of young people about the transition to secondary school and has made recommendations to policy-makers. In Scotland, Boyd and Simpson's study of S1 and S2 in one Council in Scotland demonstrated that secondary pupils have real insights to bring on a whole range of pertinent issues. Similar studies into the views of primary school pupils and of 'able' pupils told a similar story of important perspectives which if missed might render fruitless the policy-makers' best efforts.

POINTS FOR REFLECTION

1 Do we do enough to listen to the views of pupils from P6 to S2 about their experiences of school? What mechanisms could we use to give them more of a voice?

2 Do Rudduck's findings reflect the reality in your school, do you think?

3 The Boyd/Simpson study found that pupils placed a lot of importance on relationships with teachers as a pre-requisite for learning. Do you think teachers would have the same view?

4 What are your views of the homework versus work home issue as raised by parents? Is it more of an issue in secondary than primary?

8 Education 10 to 14 – new approaches needed?

> How can you get very far,
> If you don't know Who You Are?
> How can you do what you ought,
> If you don't know What You've Got?
> And if you don't know Which To Do
> Of all the things in front of you,
> Then what you'll have when you are through
> Is just a mess without a clue
> Of all the best that can come true
> If you know What and Which and Who.
>
> *Winnie the Pooh*, **A. A. Milne**

Primary–secondary transition – 'just a mess without a clue'?

It is easy to be highly critical of the current approach to primary–secondary transition. The 5–14 programme appears to have failed in at least two of its most significant objectives, namely, raising general levels of attainment and making learning progressive, continuous and coherent across P6 to S2. Secondary schools have failed to engage with 5–14 in any real sense beyond some patchy implementation of language and maths. Evaluation of the implementation of the 5–14 programme indicated that there were some successes (Boyd and Simpson 2000) but it did not make the primary–secondary curriculum a 'seamless robe' simply by describing it in the same terms within the guidelines documents. The secondary school structure remained stubbornly immune to change and concepts like environmental studies, covering up to ten secondary subjects simply never took root in the consciousness of secondary teachers or of secondary school timetablers. While there has been some recent evidence of improvement in standards nationally as measured against 5–14 levels there is no evidence of significant improvement, certainly not of the scale which would have enabled all pupils to be ready for Standard Grade exams in S3, as in the original rhetoric.

But to say that it is 'a mess' would be disingenuous. There have been a huge number of innovative strategies introduced across Scotland, some of them in terms of systems and structures, some involving bridging projects, some involving deployment of staff and others which focused on the learning and teaching process. Most primary teachers would say that 5–14 provided a welcome framework which could be applied nationwide. However, the most stringent criticism was in terms of the huge pressure to push pupils through the curriculum, to reach standards in terms of percentages of pupils achieving levels A to F and the fragmentation of the curriculum, as evidenced by the breaking up of the environmental studies guidelines into three, separate subject areas.

A final straw was national testing. Revised in the early 1990s in response to widespread professional and parental opposition to its prescriptive and judgemental nature, it became, theoretically, a set of tests in English language and maths, which the teacher would select from and use only when she was sure that the pupils were already confidently working at the particular level. The result of the test would confirm the teacher's judgement in 95 per cent of cases and if there were a discrepancy, the teacher's judgement would prevail. However, gradually the tests and the levels began to be used for purposes for which they had never been designed. Firstly, under pressure to meet targets, teachers began using the letters A to F to grade individual pieces of work, so that they would have 'evidence' should HMI call. Then, some secondary schools, under pressure to 'set' by attainment earlier and earlier, began to use 5–14 levels to allocate pupils to classes in certain subjects. Finally, primary schools also succumbed to the pressure to set, and used levels and test scores to group pupils, often across stages, for maths and possibly English language. But these tests were never designed for that purpose, and their flaws were exposed. Secondary teachers did not trust primary teachers' test scores, and primary teachers felt uneasy that their judgements were being used to set pupils in the secondary.

Notwithstanding these difficulties, there have been successful attempts made through 5–14 to achieve some measure progression, continuity and coherence across P6 to S2. In this chapter we will look at some of these, as well as looking at some of the issues which are emerging in other countries.

Re-structuring S1 and S2 – different approaches

As we have seen, the generally held view is that the problems lie in S1 and S2, though it cannot be said that 5–14 has had a wholly beneficial effect on P6 and P7 since its inception. Thus, it is not surprising that many secondary schools have tried to re-structure S1 and S2 in a variety of ways. The HMI view on S1 and S2 was that timetabling solutions could be found to the problem of pupils having too many teachers in a week. By the use of rotations and more effective timetabling of upper school classes, there should be no split classes (i.e. where two teachers share the same class because it could not be fitted into the timetable of either one) and it should be possible to reduce the number of teachers to around ten. The problem is that not all timetablers give that level of priority to S1 and S2, and principal teachers dislike rotations, because they only see classes for part of the year. These devices have had little impact on most secondary schools, and the average number of teachers seen in a week by S1 and S2 classes remains well above the target of 10. However, even within these constraints, there have been interesting attempts made to introduce change.

School A

This school had had a conventional S1 and S2 structure. The head and his senior management team were concerned about fragmentation of the curriculum, but were more worried about a falling off in motivation among S2 pupils and the beginnings of underachievement, especially among boys. After consultation with staff, the decision was taken to introduce subject choice at the end of S1, in addition to the more normal subject choice at the end of S2. Pupils could drop one of the three social subjects – history, geography or modern studies and could choose three out of five practical subjects – art, home economics, music, technology or computing.

The rationale was that pupils did not need more than two social subjects for any career path they might want to follow, and so would not be disadvantaged by dropping one. Pupils who might want to pursue a career which was leant more towards practical subjects would not be disadvantaged either, since when the S2 choice came around, after they had done the compulsory English, maths, modern language, science and social subject, they would only have room on their timetable for three practical subjects at most.

The school has operated this S1 choice strategy for a number of years and is convinced that it raises levels of pupil motivation, addresses the 'dip' in S2 where pupils, having made a choice in their own minds about subject in S2, simply switch off in the latter part of S2. Teachers in the affected subjects believe that the loss of some students, especially students with abilities in their subject, is offset by the fact the pupils have chosen to be in the subject in S2 and are more likely to work enthusiastically.

It could be argued that such an approach runs counter to the spirit of the 'common course' as envisaged by the architects of the comprehensive school. It could also be argued that S1 is too early for any meaningful or informed choice to be made. Nevertheless, this school feels that on balance the effects are positive and that it is one way of reducing fragmentation while improving pupil motivation.

School A's approach could be said to be cautious rather than radical. The system works more or less as before except that in S2 pupils are experiencing three subjects fewer than before. The approach taken to these subjects and the timetabling approaches are relatively unaltered. In School B, the approach is more radical.

School B

This is a secondary school in which some internal re-building gave the headteacher an opportunity to restructure the S1 and S2 curriculum in ways which, on the one hand preserved the best of P6 and P7 practices, and on the other tried to enable secondary teachers to work collaboratively with colleagues across the subject boundaries. There were to be S1 and S2 base areas in which classes would stay for all of the subjects which did not require specialist accommodation. Teachers would move and would teach these classes in these base areas. At the same time, the curriculum was re-organised into three broad areas: humanities; science, maths and technology; and expressive arts. Within these three areas, teachers would work in teams with a class, for a whole morning or afternoon at a time. They could work in different ways at different times, depending on the nature of the learning taking place. At one point they may be working in one, flexible semi-open plan area as team, with one taking the lead and the others supporting; at another, after a lead lesson, perhaps, they might each take a class on their own as a follow up to the work. They would have to be prepared to work on subject-matter outside their own sphere of expertise, and adapt their methodologies to suit the needs of the learners and the styles of their colleagues. The rationale was that pupils in S1 and S2 often have no sense of 'belonging' and the base areas would provide that. The three broad areas would bring coherence to the learning and would enable 'integrative experiences' to take place. Pupils would be more likely to transfer skills and to make connections in their learning. As might be anticipated, there was not unanimous support for this approach. Teachers and teaching unions objected because it was undermining the importance of the subject and perhaps threatening teachers' job prospects in the long run. The General Teaching Council expressed concerns about teachers working in areas in which they were not qualified. Parents worried about the innovative nature of the approach and the fact that it was untested. In the event, it was never fully evaluated and remains an approach which is strong on rationale but not yet able to support its claims with evidence.

It is interesting to note that School B was unique in Scotland in its innovative approach to S1 and S2. No other schools have taken such steps to restructure the curriculum, the teaching methods and the professional ways of working of teachers so radically. This may indicate that the school was well ahead of its time and that others will follow suit, albeit in different ways. Or it may mean that the idea was not well grounded and that other schools would be reluctant to depart so radically from existing approaches. Either way, there has been no rush on the part of schools in Scotland to make dramatic changes either to S1 and S2 or to the whole P6–S2 stage. Indeed, much of the recent school building projects have simply consolidated the *status quo* in terms of provision for S1 and S2 courses. It seems likely, therefore, the next phase of school buildings in the primary sector will do the same.

School C

A secondary school in the north-east of Scotland, awarded almost £200,000 by the Scottish Executive as part of the Future Learning and Teaching (FlaT) initiative, has introduced subject choice at the end of S1. Unlike School A, it has also brought forward Standard Grade so that pupils begin the two-year courses at the start of S2 and will sit the exams at the end of S3. In the same way, pupils will sit their national qualifications exams a year earlier than at present, and the plan is to use the time which is freed up at the end of the pupils' schooling to do a range of innovative courses, including Duke of Edinburgh Awards, mini-enterprise projects and other courses in partnership with the local FE college.

The schools has been mindful of the need to apply the HMI criteria for creative, innovative and flexible approaches to the curriculum:

- consultation
- focus on improving learning
- commitment to evaluation.

There was consultation with parents, primary schools, local authority, colleges and universities. The focus on learning was helped by the dropping of some of the content of the traditional S1/S2 courses and an increase in the 'pace of learning', a phrase much used by HMI in their criticism of S1 and S2 in many schools. The school did an audit of all existing S1 and S2 courses, looking for repetitions and overlaps both with P6 and P7 and among subjects in the secondary school. ICT skills were audited also, and the contribution of each subject to the development of pupil's skills was identified. Homework was also examined, and overlaps, clashes and repetitions eliminated as far as possible. A spin-off from this concentration on S1 has been the development of a 'link project' in science involving P7s in the associated primary schools.

In the first year of the initiative, there are S2 pupils and S3 pupils beginning S grade courses at the same time. In some cases they are being taught together in the same classes and the S2 pupils appear to be keeping up with their S3 counterparts. When the first cohort of pupils reaches S5 and S6, the plan is that there will a wide range of new courses, provided jointly by the school, the FE College, the community and by other organisations.

School C is one of the first in Scotland to have responded to the SEED Flexibility circular in a radical and whole-school way. It could be argued that some its plans do not go as far as those of School B some 10 years earlier. Allowing pupils to sit examinations a year earlier, for some, is the opposite of what we should be doing. Examinations and the restrictive effect they have on learning and teaching are what teachers cite most frequently when asked why they do not introduce new methods in their classroom. Will moving onto S Grade a year earlier help that situation? Time will tell; but School C is to be commended for its attempt to address some of the structural problems facing the early years of secondary school and for having consulted widely before introducing change. The question of evaluation is crucial, and it should be running parallel to the introduction of the changes, not simply carried out *post hoc*. There is an opportunity for ongoing qualitative and quantitative research to be carried out which might illuminate the successes and failures of this, or any other similar, initiative.

If the structure of the curriculum and of schools themselves is not changing, how can the issues within the 10–14 age group be addressed in different ways?

Teachers on the move: 10–14 revisited?

The scheme has been funded by SEED and is a pilot, but there are no signs that it is a model for all other clusters to follow. It does however, point in the direction of the 10–14 report at least in part. If the principle of specialist teachers in the upper primary school is agreed, then it might be argued that these teachers should be a mix of primary and secondary teachers who could work across P6 to S2. Indeed, if they were able to work as teams, they might provide some of the continuity which appears to be lacking in the current set-up. If the principle of specialism is conceded in the primary, the principle of generalism, or integrated learning, might be conceded in the secondary. Instead of fifteen subjects taught by fifteen different teachers, there might be a thematic approach where the skills and concepts would still be taught but in contexts where pupils and teachers would work in cross-curricular ways. The teams of teachers who move between primary and secondary, augmented by some of the secondary staff, would build on the learning in P6 and P7, and would make the whole experience more progressive, continuous and coherent.

It might be a little too innovative at present, but the seeds have been sown in the 10–14 report, there seems to be some nurturing of the seedlings in Highland Council, and who knows what new ideas might flourish in the near future?

Management and structures – council-wide approaches

From the perspective of a local authority, the management of primary–secondary transition can be seen as a structural issue. The cluster of schools has been recognised as an entity for planning and resources purposes for some years. In the 1980s, some divisions of Strathclyde region took a cluster approach to the allocation of some specialist staff. If the secondary had surplus staff in areas such as PE, art, music or technology, and the associated primary schools had a vacancy for part of a teacher (expressed in terms of Full Time Equivalent (FTE), e.g. 0.2 FTE would be one day per week of a teacher, and so on), then the teacher could be shared among the schools. In the same decade, schools serving 'areas of priority treatment', identified as such because of the incidence of poverty and disadvantage, had Circular 991 appointments on a cluster basis. PE was often targeted as part of the health-promoting schools initiative, and a secondary PE specialist would be appointed to the cluster and would work with all of the associated primary schools.

In the 1990s and into the twenty-first century, some of these initiatives disappeared as the funding ended, while others developed to meet new circumstances. In Glasgow, Learning Communities emerged with a single principal, drawn from the ranks of the headteachers of the schools involved. The management of the curriculum is done on a cluster basis and resources are planned jointly. In some councils, the focus is 5–14 and there are 'cluster co-ordinators' appointed from the schools in the cluster (but not at headteacher level) to promote continuity, coherence and progression across P6 to S2.

One council has proposed a cluster management structure which will see a cluster head, appointed at a salary higher than that of the secondary headteacher, and not necessarily from within the cluster itself. There will be two other senior managers for the cluster, operating between the level of primary and secondary headteacher, one with a responsibility for the curriculum and the other for pupil support. The combined salaries for these posts will be substantial, part of which may be offset by a reduced complement of centrally located staff and, in the medium term, 'job-sizing' of senior managers in the schools. The strategic aim is look at the whole of the child's experience of schooling and manage the curriculum, staffing and resources in a planned and co-ordinated way. The obvious drawback is the apparent proliferation of management posts, and the new relationship these people will have with existing headteachers, existing staff and with school boards. It seems top-heavy, and the question must be whether the same strategic aims could not be achieved with fewer management posts outside of the school structures. However, on the plus side, it is a bold attempt to look holistically at the curriculum 3–18 and how it can be most coherently managed at a local level. Time alone will tell if it successful.

Messages from research

In 2003, Maurice Galton, John Gray and Jean Rudduck from the University of Cambridge carried out research on *transfer* (from one school to another) and *transition* (from one stage to another within a school) in England. In addition, they tracked pupils in more than 300 primary schools and drew on their earlier review of the research literature (1999) which had shown that while schools' arrangements for transfer were mainly working, there was a need to understand more about the dips in attitude, engagement and progress which seemed to take place in Year 8 (S2).

Whatever the model, it is clear that the aim of introducing more continuity, coherence and progression into the present system of schooling is the key objective. However, in the 1999 review of the literature and effective practice, Galton and his team found that:

- Most of the extant research had focused on the personal and social effects of transfer.
- Despite evidence over twenty years that the transfer from primary to secondary has become less stressful for pupils, schools still put most of their effort into smoothing the process.

- Two out of every five pupils were estimated to fail to make expected progress during the year immediately following the change of schools.
- Despite the National Curriculum there are still problems at transfer with curriculum continuity ... and some secondary teachers still cling to the principle of the 'fresh start'.
- For some schools the task of managing the transfer process is made more difficult because [of] ... parental choice; many schools are dealing with large numbers of 'feeder' schools.
- Amongst the schools which have adopted more innovative approaches to transfer, most are concentrating on extended induction programmes.

(*Executive Summary*, p. ii)

The researchers went on to make a number of recommendations, including:

- More radical approaches needed which give attention to discontinuities in teaching approaches, look at the gap between pupils expectations of the next phase of schooling and the reality, and help teachers to develop strategies for helping pupils to manage their own learning.
- There is a need for more research that would plug gaps in the knowledge base (e.g. the impact of initiatives such as the literacy and numeracy strategies, summer vacation 'catch up' programmes, homework and breakfast clubs for pupils 'most at risk').
- There is a need for better baseline evidence against which the impact of various initiatives could be evaluated.
- Schools need to consider the possibility of providing flexible teaching which takes account of differences in pupils' preferred learning styles, paying particular attention to gender differences.
- As more schools seek ways of raising standards by reducing the negative imapct of transfer ... on pupil progress, it will be important to provide a record of 'successful practices' which schools can use and build on.

(*Executive Summary*, pp. ii–iii)

Four years on, the same researchers, now able to examine practice in more than 50 schools in a dozen LEAs, concluded:

Nine schools were the subject of case studies. They were chosen because Y7 pupils made significantly higher positive attitude gains after transfer compared to the remaining schools in the sample. They shared certain characteristics. Most used some form of Bridging Unit, had extended induction programmes and provided summer programmes both for gifted pupils and those needing to catch up with numeracy and literacy. Some had exchanged visits between Y6 and Y7 subject specialists. Some schools were exploring the use of the Internet for linking Y6 and Y7 pupils in 'buddying' schemes.

(p. iii)

The researchers worked in seven schools with pupils 'who have turned away from learning' and made several 'key observations':

- The process of disengagement can be reversed if pupils feel that significant others in the school are able to see and acknowledge some of their strengths.
- Anti-work identities, once established, are difficult to change and it is better to intervene early in pupils' school careers.
- Things that could make a difference for these pupils include more time in school to talk about difficulties, targets that they can identify themselves and recognition of effort and small successes.

(p. v)

Finally, in their Overall Recommendations, the authors suggest that policy-makers direct their attention to:

- The academic (as opposed to social) dimensions of transfer and the specific strategies which help sustain pupils' progress.
- The balance of pre- and post-transfer activities. The time and resources invested in post transfer activities should be designed to sustain the excitement of learning and to help pupils to develop a language for thinking and talking about their learning.

These issues might well have come from a Scottish study, and they remind us of the need to find robust ways of evaluating the impact of initiatives, to focus on ensuring that learning is progressive and continuous, and to share good practices as widely as possible.

SUMMARY

At the early part of the twenty-first century, a consensus is emerging that the 5–14 programme, while successful in offering a broad curricular framework, has not fulfilled the aims set out by politicians in the 1980s of raising attainment for all and delivering progression, coherence and continuity (with even breadth and balance having some negative impact). Recently, individual schools have tried to address the problems of S1 and S2 with interesting results, but the picture nationally is patchy. Some councils have taken imaginative steps to address the problems of curricular discontinuity, either through teams of teachers working across the sectors, or by creating new cluster-based management structures. In England, research has indicated that some of the efforts around transition can be misplaced if they do not have a clear focus on the curriculum and on the process of learning how to learn (metacognition).

POINTS FOR REFLECTION

1 What do you see as the main advantages and disadvantages of School A's approach? Is earlier choice helpful in dealing with pupil motivation?

2 School B's approach is radical, at least in the Scottish context. Is it too radical?

3 Bringing forward the date of presentation for national examinations is becoming a popular way of meeting the needs of more able pupils. What do you think it offers the pupils? How will it impact positively on pupil learning?

4 Is the cluster the way forward? Can it deliver continuity, coherence and progression? If so, how?

9 Joined-up thinking

> Marriage is popular because it combines the maximum of temptation with the maximum of opportunity.
>
> *Marriage*, G. B Shaw

Problems are our friends

For as long as we can remember, transition from primary to secondary school has been seen as a problem to be solved. It has rarely been seen as an opportunity for creative thinking, insight or creativity. Now, there is an opportunity to look afresh at what has been happening between P6 to S2. The temptation is to do nothing, or to tinker with the *status quo*. After all, the statistics seem to suggest that pupils make up the gap in attainment which seems to appear in S1 and S2 by the time they reach S4. So, is it really a problem?

If the evidence seems to point to a worrying lack of progress in S1 and S2 based on progress between P4 and P7, then we have to assume that there is no congenital reason for it. If we accept Feuerstein's thesis that 'the chromosome does not have the last word', then we have to believe that all pupils are capable of learning. They are, as Feuerstein says, 'modifiable'; their brains can grow and develop, provided that the right 'mediation' takes place. We also know more about the learning process than we did fifteen to twenty years ago and research into how human beings learn is reaching the classroom directly, albeit in a piecemeal way.

A challenge for the education system is to ensure that all those who work with young people are exposed to this research in ways which enable them to modify their practice in the classroom. In other words, the journey from theory to practice is not a simple one, as we have seen with the *Primary Memorandum* (Chapter 2). How then can it be done?

A policy for primary education: one council's approach

In 2003, one council in Scotland launched its policy on learning and teaching in the primary school. It did so with a flourish. Over a two-day period in which all schools were closed for in-service training, it ran four conferences, two simultaneously on each day, in which all primary staff, teaching and support staff, participated. The council invited three major figures in the world of learning, teaching and continuing professional development to address the conferences, and there were workshops to enable participants to engage with the council's policy document.

A glance at the Contents page of the document shows the extent of the attempt by this council to engage staff with key ideas affecting pupils' ability to learn successfully.

CONTENTS

Young Children as Learners	1
Learning through the eyes of a young child	
How do young children learn?	
Early Intervention in Action	3
Learning in an Early Intervention classroom	
Learning devotes lots of time to the oral curriculum	
The children are surrounded by a rich learning environment	
Learning involves parents in a variety of ways	
Using Early Intervention Strategies	8
Interactive teaching	
Building upon an Early Years approach	
Using Current Research	11
Emotional Intelligence	12
Motivation	
The self-motivating classroom	
Flow	

Inside the document, there is an attempt to range over a number of theories, including multiple intelligences, emotional intelligences, 'flow', motivation, self-esteem and others. Issues such as gender and learning are tackled and there are practical ideas for Brain Gym exercises based on the work of Carla Hannaford. The style of the document is direct, visual and engaging. It presents ideas in a simple way, designed to be used in staff development contexts where teachers are working collaboratively. Practicality is its aim and the ideas are presented in such a way as to promote discussion, leading to action, once assimilation has taken place.

Flow

The American psychologist Csikszentmihalyi stated that when learners are highly motivated with tasks they find challenging yet attainable they are *in flow*.

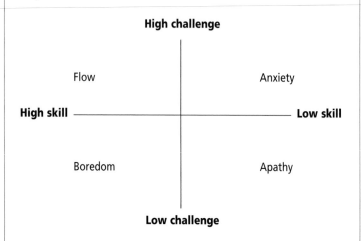

For high skill there needs to be lots of practice. When we are in flow, the time passes without our knowing it. In the time we have available to us, we have achieved something purposeful and the entire experience has been worthwhile.

We know when our children are in flow because they do not want the lesson or activity to stop, or they ask for it to be repeated. When children are in flow, the confidence increases and their self-esteem is raised.

If the document can be criticised on the grounds that it reduces individual theories to half a page and therefore removes much of the rationale underpinning each, it can be said that the cumulative effect is a consistently positive message about the possibility of effective learning for all pupils.

In one page, the reader is introduced to the idea of right and left brain functions, the triune 'three part' brain and the functions of each part, the pathways to the brain and the goal of 'whole-brain' learning. However, aware of the possibility of overload, the authors of the document then presented three pages of 'Strategies to develop whole-brain learning'.

Strategies to develop whole-brain learning

Fact
We learn best when we are confident, challenged but relaxed.

Strategy
Create a calm, positive atmosphere where children are keen to have a go without being scared to make mistakes. Use routines to prepare children for learning to come. Music can be used where appropriate.

Fact
We learn best when we connect the learning.

Strategy
Find out what the learners already know and what they need to know. Some of our children don't see the connections in learning, and subsequently it has no relevance to them. By using analogies like 'it's like when…', helps them to make connections.

Fact
Many learners cannot learn if they do not know what to expect and what is to follow.

Strategy
Share the Big Picture. Just two minutes at the beginning of the lesson sharing the purpose of the lesson with children will help connect and create a purpose for the learning.

Fact
We know that the brain learns best in chunks. At the early stages this will be within two minutes of the child's chronological age, e.g. at age five, this would be within three and seven minutes.

Strategy
Chunk the learning into sections according to the age/stage of the children. Create periods in between for the learners to talk about and share the learning. Create Brain Breaks and then re-focus. Brain Breaks may take many forms. They can involve children in some form of movement, a Brain Gym exercise, drinking water, telling a joke or having a minute to talk to a neighbour.

Fact
We learn more at the beginning and end of a lesson, but sometimes lose the middle section.

Strategy
Create lots of beginnings and endings in your lessons. Chunking the lesson creates this effect. This strategy is particularly successful for boys and keeps their learning focused.

Fact

Scientists have found a neural link between areas of the brain involved with movement and those involved with thinking.

Strategy

Use movement to anchor thoughts and build nerve networks. Movement can take many forms:

- Writing – the very act of moving your hand when writing allows thought connections to be made. This could take the form of Mind Mapping or note taking.
- Talking – allowing children many opportunities to share their learning with a partner, a group or the class helps to reinforce learning.
- Cross-lateral movements – these movements, as in Brain Gym's Cross Crawls, allows us to access both brain hemispheres simultaneously.
- Co-ordinated movements – simple muscular activities as in 'The Class Moved' or Tai-Chi, help to increase the numbers of neural connections in the brain.
- Raps – apart from the fun aspects, whole-brain learning takes place, as both hemispheres of the brain are in operation.
- Sucking – there is current evidence to show that the sucking action activates certain areas of the brain, which aids learning.

Fact

We remember the context of the learning more than the content.

Strategy

Try to link important information and concepts to something emotive, dramatic or unexpected. As adults, most of our significant memories of childhood will have emotive connections.

Fact

Recall is dramatically improved when information is reviewed. Trying to learn without review is like trying to fill the bath without putting the plug in.

Strategy

Build review into our learning. Tell your neighbour about what you have just learned. Look at the original learning outcomes, use learning maps to go over the key points and show children how this will link into the next session of work to follow.

It is a bold attempt on the part of this authority to distil much of the recent research and thinking about learning into an accessible document and to support its introduction with high quality CPD.

A tapestry of learning – a secondary schools initiative

One local authority has chosen to concentrate on the secondary sector and has launched a Creative Learning Initiative in partnership with an organisation called *Tapestry*. The authority is building on work which has been started as part of its focus on learning and teaching, and it has seconded a member of staff from one of its schools to lead the initiative. *Tapestry*'s contribution is to bring leading edge thinkers and writers on education, such as Howard Gardner, Tony Buzan, Reuven Feuerstein, Carla Hannaford, David Perkins and Mihaly Csikszentmihalyi to Scotland, to work with them in developing training materials for schools and to form a partnership with the authority in bringing this work to every teacher and support worker in every school.

In addition, over a period of three weeks, every secondary school received in-service training to support the initiative. The authority's learning and teaching group has prepared a leaflet for every teacher which outlines the key areas which the initiative will cover, but each school is invited to decide on the specific aspect on which it will focus.

What is unique about the initiative is not simply the partnership approach nor the coverage of every school simultaneously, but the fact that the timescale is three years. This is not about 'quick fixes' but is an attempt to develop the expertise, confidence and competence of every member of staff and to enable them to work together collaboratively across subjects to promote effective learning and teaching for all.

Each secondary school's entire staff has signed up to a half-day's in-service on new approaches to learning and teaching, with a specific council emphasis on emotional intelligence. In addition, a member of staff was seconded to work on the production of a *Tapestry* module aimed at the chartered teacher programme and available to all interested staff. For those who are not inclined to pursue the chartered teacher route, there will

IN–SERVICE by Dr Brian Boyd 2003/2004

Self esteem and emotional learning
- Understanding how emotions affect learning.
- Recognising emotional state of learning.
- Removing emotional blocks to learning.

Emotions and learning
- Emotions have a direct impact on ability to memorise.
- Emotions affect learning in every lesson taught.
- Emotions affect your ability to meet goals.
- An appropriate emotional climate is indispensable to sound education.

Self-esteem
- Self image everything about you and how you relate to others.
- Self image can change.
- Learning becomes valuable if you see yourself and others as valuable.

Aim   Teaching for Learning and Raising Attainment for all; reducing the attaintment gap by overcoming barriers to learning.

Rationale Effective Teaching for Learning is crucial to raising attainment. The In-Service is designed to buld upon known techniques and associated strategies of effective learning and teaching and to help teachers create conditions so that pupils will experience success through enhanced self-belief.

Teachers will be provided with the opportunity to:

- think about themselves as **learners**
- focus on factors which influence **success** and **attainment**
- focus on factors over which teachers have **control**
- improve the understanding of the pace of **emotions** in learning
- place **valuing** individuals at the heart of learning and teaching
- develop **confidence-building** of pupils into each course.

Follow-on work will be organised in school and across schools to allow teachers to:

- work in partnerships
- observe others teaching
- plan implementation
- deal with low level disruption.

Teaching for Learning and Raising Attainment for All
In-Service Dr B Boyd
Self Esteem and Emotional Intelligence

In School Programme 2004–2006
- Management of learning.
- Creating a supportive climate for learning.
- Interactive teaching.
- Teaching and learning styles.

Characteristics of disaffected pupils
- Low self esteem
- Can be defensively confrontational
- Need lots of praise and encouragement
- Need teachers who are:
  - i   decisive
  - ii   confident
  - iii   firm
  - iv   fair
  - v   able to avoid confrontations
  - vi   show every person respect
  - vii   do not use sarcasm
  - viii   do not humiliate a pupil
  - ix   do not say things to them that they would never say to friends or colleagues.

Tapestry/SBC

be in-service training on aspects of 'brain-based learning' provided by Tapestry consultants initially, but in due course led by trained council staff from the advisory service and from schools.

The plan is a five-year one which is not promising quick fixes, but which is trying to build on the existing good practice within the council. The aim is to enable teachers as reflective professionals to engage with some of the new ideas in learning and teaching, and in a collaborative culture within and among schools, to share their expertise with others with a view to creating 'learning communities'. In this way the improved practice is more likely to become embedded in the culture of the school.

Thinking about learning – a joined up approach?

A third authority has focused on 'thinking skills' as a way of promoting effective learning and teaching across the whole age range. Once again a member of staff has been seconded to lead the thinking skills initiative. Here the focus has been on promoting thinking skills across the primary and secondary sectors, putting in place a range of programmes and resources which can be used from P1 (if not before) through to S6. Many of these are commercial packages and the authority has provided a grid which shows graphically at what stage the programme is best used, the kinds of thinking skills on which the programme focuses, the time required within the curriculum, the resources involved, training requirements and additional comments.

**Draft Whole School Programme
Developing Thinking**

Stage	Core Resource
P1	Let's Think! Concept Cartoons: Infant Book – The Snowman's Coat First Stories for Thinking (Philosophy with Children)
P2	Let's Think! Concept Cartoons: Infant Book – The Snowman's Coat First Stories for Thinking (Philosophy with Children)
P3	Let's Think! Concept Cartoons: Infant Book – The Snowman's Coat First Stories for Thinking (Philosophy with Children)
P4	Let's Think through Science Concept Cartoons A Guide to Better Thinking Stories for Thinking (Philosophy with Children)
P5	Let's Think through Science Concept Cartoons A Guide to Better Thinking Stories for Thinking (Philosophy with Children)

P6   Concept Cartoons
            A Guide to Better Thinking
            Stories for Thinking (Philosophy with Children)

P7   Thinking Science CASE lessons 1–8
            Concept Cartoons
            Stories for Thinking (Philosophy with Children)

S1   Thinking Science CASE lesson 9...
            Thinking Maths
            Concept Cartoons

S2   Thinking Science ... lesson 30
            Thinking Maths
            Concept Cartoons

Other resources/strategies
SLC Problem Solving pack
Formative assessment strategies
Mind Mapping

This list shows the **choices** of resources at each stage. By implementing
activities from the resource or implementing the whole resource, a
school will be able to develop a whole school approach to developing
thinking.

In addition, the authority has produced a CD-ROM which
features live-action video clips of teachers working with groups
of pupils and with whole classes, from P2 to S4. It has CPD
material to enable groups of teachers to explore how they might
use some of the approaches in their own situations.

This authority has also appointed P6–S2 co-ordinators whose
main role is to ensure that learning and teaching is progressive,
continuous and coherent; thinking skills is a key element of this
approach. In-service training goes on within the teachers' centre
and in individual schools and clusters, and the expectation is that
a thinking skills approach will begin to permeate the work of all
teachers in the authority's schools.

Lessons from abroad?

1 International comparison

In Chapter 5, we looked at some of the reasons why education has become a key political priority. In the global Village, many of these issues have a universal impact. In a *Review of Curricular Approaches in Other Countries* (2003), Appleton considered seven countries which are considered, in educational terms, as high performing, namely Canada, Finland, New Zealand, Northern Ireland, Norway, Scotland and Tasmania. The definition of high performing may be problematic for many educationists since it relies heavily on international comparative studies such as the programme for International Student Performance (PISA). Appleton acknowledges that 'one of the key problems in cross-national comparative research is the harmonization (or lack thereof) of data'. (p. 2). Nevertheless, she tries to map the similarities and differences among the countries in an attempt to discover whether Scotland is 'on the right lines.'

Findings

Curriculum content

1.1 Common basis of subjects but different emphasis, with most countries offering few common core subjects and increasing electives with age of pupils (except Finland).

1.2 New emphasis on cross-curricular issues, especially in primary education, alongside subject-specific curriculum.

1.3 Civics is an important concern across all countries, but taught as a cross-curricular issue, mainly interwoven through other subjects

1.4 Foreign language is an important element of all countries, especially because minority cultures are found in each country, and languages are being introduced earlier.

1.5 Continuous curriculum ensures smooth transition between schools in some countries, but in others a separate curriculum begins in upper secondary school.

1.6 Separate vocational/academic routes but structured within the same institutions and/or the same assessment process encourages greater participation rates beyond compulsory education.

Principles of the curriculum
2.1 All counties express an interest in providing pupils with knowledge, skills and personal development to equip them for later life in the workplace and to encourage life-long learning.

Assessment structures and methods
1.1 Combination of emphasis on national performance examinations and teacher assessed exams at both primary and secondary level, though most sit national performance tests in both primary and secondary schools (except Norway and Finland which do not hold national performance exams).
1.2 Tendency towards incremental credit systems facilitating integration of vocational and academic courses.

Curriculum responsibility
4.1 Public authorities remain responsible for basis education curriculum, although institutions are given autonomy, thereby enhancing flexibility and adaptability to the specific needs of the school.
4.2 Greater involvement of parents and pupils themselves in curriculum choice.

School organisation
1.1 Schooling everywhere characterized by same broad stages but organisation and length vary.
1.2 Where schooling starts later, pre-school education participation rates are high according to some studies, but not among this mix of countries.
1.3 School types vary between those countries with several schools attended by the student throughout the duration of studies, to those where only one school is attended (Norway and Finland).
1.4 The same classroom teacher conducts classes in the primary phase, with some specialist teachers in music, art and PE; whereas specialist subject teachers are mainly used in teaching at secondary level.

> **1.5** Streaming [sic] of classes by ability is rare in the primary stages. In the secondary stage of education, ability streaming is more commonplace.
>
> *Review of Curricular Approaches in Othere Countries*

Appleton concludes that 'Scotland has many policies in place that bear the hallmarks of good practice' (p. 14). However she singles out concerns about the transition stages of education as being a strength of the Scottish system while pointing to improve monitoring and evaluation of policies and their impact. Finally, she argues that further research is needed in 'areas such as early school starting age and citizenship' (p. 14).

2 Norway

In 1997, the Royal Ministry of Education, Research and Church Affairs, a body whose very title should act as a warning not to try to lift ideas from other countries without a clear understanding of their cultural and historical context, produced a document entitled 'Core Curriculum for primary, Secondary and Adult Education in Norway'. The presentation of the document was indicative of the approach taken. It was glossy, attractive and illustrated with photographs, woodcuts and reproductions of fine art. Its language was not that of the official publications which we have become used to in this country. Instead, it began with a statement of aims, closely linked to five education Acts, and proceeded to focus on a range of aspects of the 'human being', beginning with the 'spiritual'.

Core curriculum for primary, secondary and adult education in Norway (1997)

Introduction

The Spiritual human being
Christian and Humanistic Values
Cultural Heritage and Diversity

The creative human being
Creative Abilities
Three Traditions

A Critical sense of Judgement
Scientific Methods and the Active Pupil

The working human being
Technology and Culture
Learning and work habits
Teaching and personal initiative
From the Familiar to the Unknown
Adapted Teaching
All-Round Development
The Role of the Teacher and Educator
Teaching Ability and Active Learning
Learning as Teamwork

The liberally-educated human being
Specific Knowledge and broad frames of reference
Common References in a Specialised Society
Internationalization and the Appreciation of Tradition

The social human being
A Diversified Peer Culture
Duties and Responsibilities
Social Learning from the School Community
A Broad Context for Learning: Peer Culture, Parent Participation and
the Local Community

The environmentally aware human being
Natural Sciences, Ecology and Ethics
Human Beings, the Environment and Conflicts of Interest
Joy of Nature

The integrated human being

The opening sentence of the document sets the tone:

> The aim of education is to furnish children, young people and
> adults with the tools they need to face the tasks of life and
> surmount its challenges together with others. Education shall
> provide learners with the capability to take charge of themselves
> and their lives, as well as with the vigour and will to stand by
> others.

(p. 5)

The language, once again, may seem slightly foreign to those of us used to reading 5–14 reports or ministerial pronouncements. However, this aspirational tone is maintained throughout and the document concludes:

> The ultimate aim of education is to inspire individuals to realize their potential in ways that serve the common good; to nurture a humaneness in a society in development.
>
> (p. 40)

Such asset of aims would not have been out of place if written during the Scottish Enlightenment. Indeed, the only twentieth century report on education in Scotland which comes close to this kind of language and tone is the 1947 *Advisory Council Report*, which, ironically, was never implemented because its recommendations (including a precursor of the comprehensive school) were deemed too radical at the time.

Joining up the initiatives

As well as all of these laudable initiatives going on at a local level, there are always national initiatives which SEED sponsors in an attempt to deliver the national priorities (see Chapter 6). Thus, Assessment is for Learning, Better Behaviour; Better Learning, Enterprise Education, Citizenship, the Health Promoting School, Thinking Skills, Creativity, Early Intervention, Inclusion, ICT, not to mention the staple diet of 5–14, Standard Grade and national qualifications, all represent worthy attempts to improve learning and teaching in Scottish schools. However the net effect on classroom teachers may well be bewilderment at best and resentment at worst. How do we join up these initiatives and ensure that schools are able to make sense of the advice being given? One way is to develop a framework of principles which would enable schools to check whether the approaches they were using were in tune with what we know contributes to effective learning and teaching.

If we were to take five of the main curricular initiatives which span primary and secondary education and try to derive a common set of principles, would it help schools and teachers make sense of how to implement them in the classroom? Would it remove the pressure to be seen to be doing each one separately, in a way which could be monitored, assessed and, ultimately. 'ticked off' as having been done?

Initiative	Key themes	Underlying principles
Assessment is for Learning (AifL)	Questioning Feedback Sharing criteria Self-assessment	Formative assessment Metacognition Empowerment of learner Collaborative learning
Better Behaviour Better Learning (BB;BL)	High expectations Challenge/support Explicit goals/target Appropriate methods	High self-esteem Motivation Pupil engagement Learning styles
Thinking Skills (TS)	Critical thnking Creative thinking Problem-solving Cognitive/affective	Metacognition Making learning explicit Collaborative learning Challenge Mediation
The Health Promoting School (HPS)	Caring ethos Pupil responsibility Success orientation	Appropriate challenge Learner-centred Pupil engagement
Creativity in Education (CiE)	Creative ethos Range of methods Problem-solving Collaborative working	Self-motivation Creative dispositions Time to think

If these are indeed the key themes and underlying principles, either as stated in the documentation which accompanies the initiatives or as gleaned from supporting literature, then is it possible to reduce these to a manageable number and in a form which is helpful to schools? Would it be possible also to promote greater continuity, progression and coherence in the curriculum across the primary and secondary sectors as a consequence? One of the functions of such a framework might be to help curriculum planners, at local authority, cluster and school level to develop creative, innovative and flexible approaches to learning and teaching, without straying from the agreed principles. Thus, while systems, structures and approaches might differ from place to place across Scotland, the quality of the learning and teaching could be assured by reference to the framework. In effect, the principles would provide the entitlement for all learners and no child would be deprived of these principles, though the contexts in which they were applied might be quite different at different stages and in different parts of the country.

Classroom practices	Initiatives
Pair/group learning	AifL; TS; HPS; CiE
Taking account of learning styles	AifL; BB;BL; TS; HPS; CiE
Open-ended questions	AifL; TS; HPS; CiE
Praise; recognition of achievements	AifL; BB;BL; TS; HPS; CiE
Appropriate/high challenge and support	AifL; BB;BL; TS; HPS; CiE
Negotiating/sharing objectives	AifL; BB;BL; TS; HPS; CiE
Negotiating/making explicit criteria for success	AifL; BB;BL; TS; HPS; CiE
Structures teacher mediation of pupil learning	BB;BL; TS
Peer and self-assessment	AifL; BB;BL; TS; HPS
Pupil self-motivation	AifL; BB;BL; TS; HPS; CiE
Time for thinking	AifL; BB;BL; TS; HPS; CiE
Positive classroom climate/ethos	AifL; BB;BL; TS; HPS; CiE

Even a general attempt such as this to look at how teaching and learning approaches can contribute to more than one of these initiatives would suggest that there are core elements of effective classroom practice which should be encouraged in primary and secondary schools. It could be argued that even the *Classroom practices* above which do not appear to relate to specific initiatives, probably do if we look more closely at the underlying principles. It is likely that they are simply not explicitly stated. In other words, we appear to be close to a consensus on the elements which contribute to effective learning across primary and secondary schools. It is these which might offer the solution to continuity, coherence and progression.

The obvious problem with such an approach is that the framework of principles must be such that it is neither so detailed as to become a straitjacket, nor so vague and general that it becomes a licence to do anything. It should provide a safeguard that all pupils have a high quality of learning and teaching, while meething their changing needs at different times in their school lives.

The Learning Classroom

When Boyd and Simpson (2000) produced their report on learning and teaching in S1 and S2 in Angus Council schools, they included a table entitled *Towards the Learning Classroom*. This was an attempt to derive from observed lessons a set of principles which might help schools in their efforts to monitor classroom practice, through teachers' shared observation of one another's lessons.

Towards the Learning Classroom

Develop a set of principles associated with:	Consider these issues and questions amongst others	Consider these issues and consult these sources of information
The promotion of an ethos of achievement and commitment	Are pupils' assisted to set high targets and see achieving these as a joint enterprise with the teacher? Are pupils helped to identify why they are not achieving well at something? Are pupils in S1/2 brought into contact with good role models from 5th and 6th year? Do all pupils feel that their achievements are valued? What do teachers see is the main obstacle to achieving better attitudes and achievement in their classes? Why might some pupils not be motivated as much as they should be? Are pupils proud to be in your school? Are teachers proud of their school? 'I spend most of my time fighting disappointment.'	1 The use of praise (SCCC) 2 Case studies (SNAP) 3 Listening to pupils' voices

The key aspects of your model of learning	'Talking with colleagues is the best type of in-service.' If this is the best way for teachers to learn, could it also be true of pupils? Do pupils get opportunities to talk together and 'brainstorm' over a work related problem? 'Telling someone is the worst way of teaching something.' How does your normal method of teaching fit with the views of this teacher? Is giving back marks an adequate form of feedback for a pupil to improve their learning? How do teachers help pupils to see how best to learn something? How can teachers get access to the rich knowledge which pupils bring to their subject learning? Are pupils aware of the purposes of their learning and how to evaluate their own effectiveness? Do teachers know what pupils think is the work of which they are proudest? Share with colleagues an instance of pupils really surprising you with what they had produced.	4 Differentiation (M Simpson) 5 Achieving Success in S1 and S2 (HMI) 6 Teaching for Effective Learning
How the learning and teaching policy will underpin all other policies	How does homework help to enhance learning? Will attendance improve if teachers and learners find classrooms happier and more enjoyable places to be? 'They are a difficult class but they even came in at lunchtimes to finish off the work' Can finding a good way of promoting a topic have a significant effect on motivation and hence discipline? How does the policy on praise and reward link with the school's attempts to raise attainment?	7 Schools Speak for Themselves (article) 8 Schools Speak for Themselves (extract)

	Is the school timetable ever subjected to analysis in terms of its impact on learning and teaching? What is the school's policy on punishment exercises and what implicit messages does it send about certain types of tasks?	
The contribution of Learning Support	'I have much more impact if I work with staff than if I work with individual pupils' Is the experience which support for learning staff have, through visiting classrooms, shared with colleagues as part of staff development? Is there time for support for learning teachers to pre-plan and, on occasions, 'debrief' with co-operative teachers? Is the role of the support teacher in the classroom understood by the class teacher – and by the pupils? Is there any evaluation of the impact of support for learning on pupil attainment? Do the benefits of having small, lower sets, with the presence of a support teacher outweigh the evidence that setting may depress self-esteem and attainment among lower set pupils?	9 Paul Hamill (article) 10 Kings College paper on setting in Maths
Teaching methodology	Is every teacher aware of the range of successful teaching methods in this school? Are there mechanisms for the sharing of good practice among teachers? Do teachers, within and across departments, get opportunities in a focused way to observe colleagues teacher and/or to shadow pupils? Are teaching methods – across the curriculum – weighted towards teacher-led, didactic approaches?	11 Differentiation (MS) 12 Classroom observation (extract) 13 Extension Article

	Are pupils ever involved in discussing or even choosing the preferred learning/teaching approach? Are able pupil pupils challenged sufficiently, whether in set or mixed ability classes?	
The promotion of responsibility and independence in learners	Do secondary teachers know what pupils can do when they arrive from P7? Are pupils introduced to a range of metacognitive strategies to enable them to become more independent as learners? Is there a core of such strategies in use which all teachers reinforce across the curriculum when appropraite? Do more able pupils get meaningful tasks to do if and when they finish early? Are thinking skills – such as those embedded in CASE – developed in classrooms across the curriculum? Is collaborative learning used as a core strategy?	14 Thinking Skills (article) 15 Nisbet 16 Fisher
The use of resources	How are teachers allocated to classes in S1 and S2? Are S1 and S2 added into the timetable after S3 to S6 is complete? If so, what principles underpin the S1 and S2 timetable? How is *per capita* allocated across departments and within departments to ensure that S1 and S2 is given its proper allocation? Do pupils in S1 and S2 use ICT on a regular basis in subject classrooms? Do S1 and S2 pupils regularly take books/work home to enable parents to take an interest in what they are doing?	17 Learning styles (in SCCC) 18 Achieving success in S1 and S2 (HMI) 19 SCCC Guidelines

The curriculum	Is there discussion about the contribution which individual subjects make to the overall learning experience of S1 and S2 pupils? Is there regular review of the individual elements of the curriculum and is there an overview taken of the themes, topics and skills which pupils in S1 and S2 are covering across a term/ year? Is there anyone or any group of staff with responsiliby for the coherence of the S1 and S2 curricular experience which pupils have? Is rotation used to reduce the number of class/teacher contacts in the week and, if so, how is it evaluated? How does the secondary school know if pupils in S1 and S2 are still covering skills/content/concepts which they have encountered or mastered in the primary school?	20 Practical Guides? 21 Achieving Success in S1 and S2 22 Relevanr HMI subject reports
Class organisation	Are decisions about class organisation – mixed ability, setting, broad banding, etc. – linked to the aims and puposes of learning or are they based on ideology or orthodoxy? Is there a clear rationale for the organisation of classes in S1 and S2 and is there evidence gathered of the impact on pupil achievement, the range of teaching methods and teacher expectations? What criteria are used to set or broadband pupils? Is the achievement of pupils in different sets monitored and if so what conclusions are drawn from evidence that pupils have been misplaced?	23 Two research articles 24 Achieving Success in S1 and S2 25 TESS articles or Kings College article

	Does pupil movement 'up' or 'down' in sets happen regulary? If so, what impact, if any, does it have on class-teacher continuity? Are pupils' views sought regulary on their experience of mixed ability, setting, broad banding? Are parents informed or involved in decisions about setting?	
The contribution of others in the school	In the school as a learning centre, are there opportunities for all members to make a contribution to the development of pupils' learning? In particular, what part do support staff, parents and the pupils themselves have to play in helping others to learn effectively? Has there been a recent 'audit' of the skills which these groups have so that their contribution is planned and effective? How does the school help parents to help their children to be effective learners? Are their metacognitive strategies explained to parents in ways which would enable them to support their pupils' learning? Are parents involved in the writing of curriculum/support materials for other parents?	26 Children, families and learning (extract) 27 Something on peer learning? 28 Cooper and Boyd article
The assessment and recording of pupil attainment	Is the 5–14 assessment and reporting guidelines advice in terms of assessing, recording and reporting pupil achievements discussed with departments? Is the rationale for most assessment the improvement of pupil learning? Is the underlying principle of the 5–14 assessment guideline, i.e. 'that which is necessary', applied to the advice given to teachers on assessment, recording and reporting?	29 Assessment 5–14 30 Climate for Learning (SCCC) 31 Simpson

	Is the burden of assessment on teachers and pupils commensurate with the positive impact on pupil learning? Is pupil self-assessment an integral part of school policy? Is peer assessment embedded in classroom practice?	
Using ICT	Is ICT considered to be a tool for learning or an end in itself? Are pupils using new techonology in their everyday classroom work and not simply as a separate, discreet activity in a computer suite? How, and how often, do pupils use new technology as a tool for learning? What kids of skills audits are carried out among P7 pupils before transfer to secondary? Are teachers sufficiently skilled/ confident to support pupils in their use of ICT as a learning tool?	
Classroom layout	Is the physical layout of your room (or those in your department) attractive, relevant and purposeful? Are wall displays, arrangement of furniture and provision of learning resources related to the purpose of the learning? Does staff development allow teachers to share ideas on, and discuss the efficacy of, different approaches to classrrom layout? How are teachers who are peripatetic supported in their efforts to create an attractive learning environment? What is the role of the timetable in helping S1 and S2 classes to have the best and most settled experience of classroom learning?	32 Climate for Learning (SCCC) 33 Boyd (Group work) extract 34 Ruddock

A number of schools have used the table as a starting point in their efforts to use classroom observation as a strategy to empower teachers in improving learning and teaching. Some schools, notably Mossneuk Primary and Carnoustie High Schools, have used other starting points to produce *How good is my classroom* grids, derived in part from HMI documentation and from their own internal CPD.

In the past it was assumed that primary and secondary classrooms were too different (for the reasons outlined in Chapter 1) to apply the same sets of principles. However, it could be argued that the differences have always been more apparent than real and that now, as our thinking about effective learning has developed over recent years, it is the classroom which offers the most productive common ground on which primary and secondary teachers can discuss pupil progress.

SUMMARY

Some councils have taken imaginative steps to produce joined-up policies on learning and teaching. One has produced a policy on learning in the primary school based on much of the new research on the brain and on intelligences. Another has worked with an external organisation to bring similar ideas to all of its secondary schools. A third has used thinking skills as a way of trying to create coherence and progression across the sectors. Other countries have some at the same problems from slightly different perspectives. Two possible solutions are offered to the problem of fragmentation; one is by trying to elicit the key principles of the various initiatives around at any one time and using them to build up a model of effective classroom learning, while another is about looking at what teachers do in their classrooms and building up a framework for the 'learning classroom'. By so doing, it may become clear that the similarities between primary and secondary classrooms are greater than the differences.

POINTS FOR REFLECTION

1 What do you think of the council's Policy Paper for Primary Education? Is it innovative and stimulating or is it too theoretical and unrealistic for classroom teachers?

2 The *Tapestry* partnership with another council is focused on the secondary schools and seeks to bring cutting edge thinking into the classroom. What are its chances of success in your view?

3 What do you think of the approaches taken in other countries? For example, are there elements of the Norwegian system which might be applied here in Scotland?

4 Is there a need to join up the initiatives? Would it be a help to schools? What form should it take?

10 Looking back – looking forward

> 'Have we reached the end?' asked Piglet.
> 'Yes.' I replied.
> 'It seems to be the end,' said Pooh.
> 'It does. And yet–'
> 'Yes. Piglet?'
> 'For me, it also seems like a beginning.'
> *Winnie the Pooh*, A. A. Milne

Curriculum 3–18

There are many transitions in education, just as there are in life. They are all endings and they are beginnings too. A life which was unerringly smooth, with no ups and downs, would be dull indeed. And yet, if the discontinuities are too great, too traumatic and too final, then the losses may be irreparable, at least in the short term.

Is the possibility of a curriculum 3–18 a real one? If so, how can it avoid the danger of being too vague, too general and almost irrelevant? And, in trying to avoid this danger, could it be too prescriptive, too centralist and too inflexible? In the 1990s, Scotland, unlike England and Wales, did not introduce a National Curriculum which had the force of stature behind it. While the *Curriculum and Assessment: a Policy for the 90s* paper did carry within it implicit threats of central intervention should improvements not be forthcoming, the 5–14 programme was based on *Guidelines*, albeit of a highly prescriptive nature. But, ultimately a key part of the programme failed, namely the attempt by calling it 5–14 and thus spanning primary and secondary schools, to deliver continuity, coherence and progression in pupil learning. Simply ignoring the differences in curriculum structure between primary and secondary schools and assuming that, for example, something called environmental studies would bring together physics, chemistry, biology, history, geography, modern studies, home economics, technology and possible a few other subjects into a coherent subject area, was never going to be successful. History was against it; professional 'boundary maintenance' was against it; and timetabling structures in secondary schools were never going to be flexible enough, given the S1 and S2 are always timetabled last anyway.

So, if attempts since the Second World War to review slices of the system have not succeeded in dealing with the discontinuities, will the Curriculum review 3–18 fare any better?

Curriculum Reviews in Scotland since 1965

1965	Primary Memorandum	
		Secondary Comprehensive Schools
1977	Secondary 3 and 4	
	Munn report	Curriculum
	Dunning report	Assessment and Certification
	Pack Report	Truancy and Indiscipline
1978	Secondary	(Learning Difficulties)
1981	16+ Action Plan	S5 and S6
1986	10–14	Primary–Secondary Transition
1987	5–14	Primary and Early Secondary
1996	16+	Howie Report S5 and S6
1997		Early Intervention Pre–Five and Early Primary
		Curriculum Framework for Children in Pre-school years
1999	16+	Higher Still – Opportunity for All S5 and S6

The child at the centre?

One way of trying to unite the curriculum 3–18, spanning as it does pre–five to post-16, is to look at the child as a learner being at the centre. If we see this as a Mind Map, there might be a number of major branches spreading out from the child, each illustrating the kinds of capacities which should be developed. An early draft of the Curriculum Review Group's deliberations opted to represent its ideas in a series of boxes.

Successful learner

With:
- enthusiasm for learning
- determination to reach high standards of achievement
- openness to new thinking and ideas

And able to:
- use literacy, communication and numeracy skills
- use technology for learning
- think creatively and independently
- make reasoned evaluations
- apply different kinds of learning strategies in investigations.

Confident individual

With:
- self respect
- a sense of physical, mental and emotional wellbeing
- secure values and beliefs

And able to:
- relate to others and manage themselves
- pursue a healthy and active lifestyle
- be self aware
- live independently
- assess risk and take informed decisions
- achieve success in different ways.

Responsible citizens

With:
- respect for others
- commintment to participate responsibly in political, economic and cultural life

And able to:

- be knowledgeable about the world and Scotland's place in it
- evaluate scientific and technlogical issues
- understand different beliefs and cultures
- develop informed views of current issues
- make informed choices and decisions.

Effective contributors

With:
- an enterprising attitude
- resilience
- self-reliance

And able to:
- communicate in different settings
- work in partnerships and in teams
- take the intiative and lead
- apply critical thinking in new contexts
- be creative
- solve problems.

This model tries to outline the kinds of characteristics which young people in Scotland would have the opportunity to develop through the curriculum, and a range of thngs it would enable them to do as a result.

Capability – 'chromosomes do not have the last word'

This model would start from the belief, articulated by Professor Reuven Feuerstein (1990), that all human beings are capable of being successful learners. The human brain is 'plastic' and 'modifiable' and irrespective of genetic factors, the child can, through *instrumental enrichment*, be guided towards improvement as a learner. Gardner tells us that we all have 'multiple intelligences'

(1993) and that these can be used as entry points into the learning process, while Buzan reminds us of the huge, untapped potential of the human brain (2001). Goleman (1996) and Hannaford (1995) argue that the emotions and the human body itself may have as much to do with being a successful learner as the brain does. Kolb and others (1977) have pointed ot that preferred learning styles vary from person to person, and Sperry has shown how the brain itself has various loci for different processes (1968). The sum total of this knowledge is to convince teachers and others who work within the learning sphere that we should be 'optimistic' (Feuerstein) about the capability of humans to be successful learners, and that we should be very loathe to come to conclusions about the humans cannot achieve on the basis of something called 'intelligence' (Gardner).

However, there are barriers to learning, and these need to be overcome. Sometimes they stem from lack of proper nurture, from an absence of love and care, from congenital problems or from social and economic disadvantage. Often, by the time young people arrive at the formal education system, they are already well behind their peers in terms of attainment, self-efficacy and aspirations. In some cases the family is itself dysfunctional and there may be little or no belief in the power of education to transform lives or open up possibilities. The most basic mores may not have been inculcated in the child, and patterns of behaviour may be antithetical to successful learning. All of this makes the job of the educator more difficult and challenging, and the twin aims of tackling social exclusion and raising achievement can seem mutually exclusive. However, if we maintain a belief in the capability of all human beings to learn successfully, we need to be committed to that goal, and we need to embrace strategies which will help us achieve it.

Present and future needs – 'education is about preparing young people for life'

If meeting young people's present needs is a challenge, how can we even begin to meet their future needs? The pace of change in the twenty-first century will almost certainly outstrip that of the twentieth, and in the first few years of this century we have seen ample evidence of new political, technological and economic trends. A new 'world order' is the phrase that slips off the tongue of many politicians and commentators, and our education system needs to try to prepare young people for these changes. At the same time, for all young people, the present is the only reality. They have needs and desires and they want them fulfilled, now! So the education system is destined to exist in a time warp, where the present structures with its subjects, examinations and extra-curricular activities must, in some way, prepare the young people to take their place in the brave new world which has yet to materialise.

Not only that, but there are competing claims made on the education system by a range of 'end-users'. Parents, employers, politicians, church leaders, business and commerce and educationists all see the process and the product of education in slightly different ways. Young people are, variously, potential consumers, employees, parishioners, voters and learners. Paradoxically, from the point of view of socity in general, young people are increasingly seen as problems, and, as a legislation is introduced to curb anti-social behaviour, it is easy to demonise the young and seek to restrict them within society.

The so-called generation gap is alive and well in schools up and down the country. If all we did was to list the various things and activities beloved by young people which schools have tried to ban over the years, we would exemplify the gap. From long sideburns (boys) and mini-skirts (girls) in the '60s, platform shoes (both) in the '70s, personal stereos (both) in the '80s, body piercing (both) of various kinds in the '90s to mobile phones (both) in the early part of the twenty-first century – the list is almost endless. Add to this topical list of the hardy perennials of long hair (boys), make-up (girls but in some cases boys too), various adaptations of the humble neck-tie (short, long, fat, thin and so on) and various 'sporting' activities from push ha' penny to various commercial card games, and the gap is almost unbridgeable. And we have not even mentioned allegiance to various types of rock and pop music, from Goths to Neds. But, facetious and ludicrous though this sounds, there is a serious side to the generation gap.

The research evidence seems to suggest that it is at the transition from primary to secondary that young people begin to feel less like participants in than victims of education. Not only do they have fewer responsibilities given to them in the secondary school but the structures are already in place and they, as it seems to them, have to fit in. Subject choice, from S2 to S3, throws this into sharp relief when option columns appear to have been decided, irrespective of what the actual pupils wish to choose. The teaching methods may appear dull, teacher-dominated and even pointless, but the fact is that, historically, pupils are rarely let into the secret of what they are going to be learning, why they are going to learn it and how they will know if they are improving. There is evidence that things are changing, and initiatives like *Assessment is for Learning* are highlighting the need to involve pupils fully in their own learning and in the assessment of their own work.

However, the gap remains in the area of social education where young people theoretically should habe the opportunity to learn about things which affect their lives now and in the future. Sex, health and wellbeing, drugs, employment, child-rearing and managing money are only few of the topics which ought to bridge the gap between the now and the future. And yet as Boyd and Lawson (2003) have discovered, most young people do not believe tha teachers are the best people to teach them about these subjects.

Add to this the constant pressure to pass examinations and to value subjects which are deemed academic over those which are practical, then it is easy to see why schools are not meeting the needs of a substantial proportion of young people. Even those who are successful at school, and who gain the ultimate prize of five Highers at A band 1; are they being well served? Is the emphasis on passing exams inimical to real, deep, life-long learning? Will schools have inculcated in them a love of learning and a desire to continue learning, or will they drop certain subjects as soon as they leave school, and forever more see learning as a purely instrumental activity geared towards exam success? And if schools give the impression that they are in the business of 'knowledge transmisson' while unaware of the fact that some of this knowledge to be obsolete in ten or twenty years' time, young people may fail to see the point of the exercise.

Curriculum principles

We have already seen how other countries have developed their own sets of principles on which to base their curricula. Here in Scotland, just as the system has tended to address slices of the schools system in isolation, so too have different sets of principles emerged, sometimes overlapping, sometimes conflicting and often repetitious.

Thus, it could be argues that over the last 25 years, in which time the curriculum has been reviewed for early years, 5–14, S3 and S4 and post-16, as well as for pupils with additional support needs, a set of key principles have emerged:

- breadth
- balance
- continuity
- coherence
- progression
- choice
- depth
- relevance.

In addition, related issues, but perhaps not quite curricular principles, include:

recognising achievement
raising attainment
social inclusion
challenge
enjoyment.

Finally, a key idea has emerged at the highest political level, and that is *individualisation* or *personalisation*. This involves meeting the needs of the individual pupil but without sacrificing the social and collective aspects of schooling.

To complicate things further, a number of key initiatives have emerged which contain key themes of their own. They are based on underlying principles, including:

- metacognition
- co-operative learning
- formative assessment
- creativity
- tolerance
- respect for others
- risk-taking
- problem-solving.

All of this presupposes that there will be a concern to promote:

- literacy
- numeracy
- communication
- cultural heritage
- ICT.

It is clear that to reduce these lists to one, short set of principles is no easy task, particularly since some of the principles can be seen as contradictory; for example:

- balance and choice
- breadth and depth
- individualisation and co-operation.

Thus, if a single set of principles is to underpin the curriculum, they may have to be expressed in terms which make their meaning clear and make connections among them.

Content and entitlement

The content of the present curriculum can be seen as representing the best efforts of concerned educationalists to ensure that the fundamental building blocks of an educated person are in place. It could also be seen as a selection from the culture of our society or as a preparation for the world of work. What is true is that no curriculum is value-free, fixed or immutable; every curriculum changes over time, and there are competing claims on it from pupils, parents, employers and society in general. Thus deciding at any one time what the content of the curriculum should be is fraught with difficulty and subject to the pressures of various interest groups.

Without looking back through history to chart the changes in the curriculum, it could be said that there arise, from time to time, litmus tests of the curriculum. In 2004 alone, the following issues have arisen which impact on curriculum principles:

- The decision that the University of Strathclyde's Faculty of Education will not take on any Classics graduates in session 2004/2005.
- The announcement attributed (wrongly, it transpired) to the Minister that all children should do two hours per day of physical activity.
- The decision by a school in Glasgow to introduce vocational courses in the area of shipbuilding for some of its pupils.
- The decision by SEED not to collect nationally the results of 5–14 national testing.
- The decision by a secondary school to omit History from the curriculum.

How should these be interpreted? What kind of principles would need to be in pace to allow judgements to be made on the legitimacy of these decisions?

Classics

It could be added that Classics is at the heart of our European cultural heritage. Linguistically, Latin amd Greek have had a huge influence on English speakers and our literary tradition is hugely influenced by Classics also. Politically, there is an issue of choice. If there are pupils who wish to study Classics in the comprehensive system but cannot, while in the independent system it remains a compulsory subject, what effect does that have on equality of opportunity? The captains of industry and decision-makers (and their sons and daughters) may have a Classical education, it would appear, but the children of the workers may not.

PE

In an age where obesity is a real threat to the health of the nation, two hours of physical activity must, surely, be a good thing. But, if the curriculum is already overcrowded, where is the time to be found? If some children are already exceeding the minimum because of their out-of-school activities, do they need to take part in in-school PE? And what counts as physical activity? If this entitlement is to be seen as compulsion, what will it do for those young people not inclined towards sport, for example? Are we to force them because sport is 'character-building'?

Vocational education

There is nothing new in the concept of vocational education. In the 1970s, many secondary schools had Brunton Wings which were designed to allow boys (and girls in some cases) to pursue craft courses including painting, decorating and car mechanics. Prior to that, pupils were selected at age eleven or twelve years to go to senior or junior secondaries, the latter being for 'non-academic' pupils. And herein lies the dilemma. How can we ensure that there is parity of esteem between academic and vocational pathways? Indeed, can such a simple distinction be drawn? If a pupil goes to university to study law, is it a vocational or an academic course? The real danger is that if the 'less able' are encouraged to follow vocational courses and the 'more able' to do academic courses, are we in danger of re-creating junior and senior secondaries? Can all pupils be given the opportunity to do whatever mix of courses they desire?

5–14 testing and national qualifications

These tests have become unpopular largely because they have been abused. Ever since the outcry from parents and local authorities in the early 1990s when Michael Forsyth, the Education Minister, tried to impose 'primary tests' in a draconian and insensitive manner, they have been a source of concern. Used properly, the tests should only be applied by class teachers as and when individual pupils are deemed to be working confidently at a given level. If in the event, the pupil were not to do as expected in the test, for whatever reason, the judgement of the teacher was to be accepted. However, over the years, the test began to be administered, especially in secondaries, to whole year groups, under exam conditions. Eventually too, the results were used to set pupils into classes – an outcome never intended when the tests were introduced. In addition, the setting or national targets and publication of results by school and local authority 'upped the ante'. So, now that the Scottish Executive may be about to stop gathering data, will the tests stop being used, or will they revert to their original, benign use?

One local authority has proposed that P7 pupils should sit SQA Intermediate 1 exams in computing and science as a way of motivating them. This raises some important issues of principle. Is *extrinsic* motivation of the kind which works for some young people what we should be introducing into the system (in this case, into the primary school)? Is it not better to foster *intrinsic* motivation, where the child, as Csikszentmihalyi suggests (see Chapter 9) derived motivation from engagement with the task? Should we impose external, national examinations on pupils earlier and earlier, thus running the risk of narrowing the curriculum and forcing teachers to teach to the test? Would the principle of learning which is motivating, challenging, engaging and creative be stronger that that which sees external certification as the end point? Should schools be promoting deep or surface learning, and how do examinations impact on the goal? Should young people sit exams as early as possible or as late as necessary?

History

It could be argued that history is a core subject because it is essential for citizens of any country to know their past. Young people should be aware of the ideas, the events, the social movements which have shaped their country. They should know how the different peoples who make up the present population have come to be here and the contributions they have made. They should know about the impact which Scots have made on the world, for good and ill, and so on. How can this be done except through the subject known as history? It could be argued that all of this could be achieved through a cross-curricular approach, as in the case in the 5–14 subject area of environmental studies. However, the question would arise as to why history should disappear if, say, geography and modern studies are to stay. If this headteacher was saying that all of the S1 and S2 curriculum should be taught in a cross-curricular way, building on the link with P7, there would be a logic. If he is saying that he is simply 'dropping' history because it is not relevant or popular or important, it would be quite another matter.

The key to resolving such contentious issues is surely a clear set of principles underpinning any curricular choices which heads, teachers or pupils make. The task of the ministerial review group, therefore, is not to champion any one subject over any other, but to give guidance at the level of curriculum principles so that those who plan the curriculum, nationally and locally, do so in a reasoned way.

Outcomes

So what outcome do we wish to achieve at various stages in our educational system? Up until now, we have tended to focus on the measurable – exam results, test scores, attendance and exclusion rates and leaver destinations. These are all *products*. Should we be concentrating more on *processes* and *experiences*? At Birmingham LEA, under the leadership of Professor Tim Brighouse, the education system identified a set of experiential outcomes, such as taking part in a public performance, experiencing a residential stay or producing something using IT, as legitimate outcomes for all young people. Can we do the same? And can we set out the principles in such a way that schools can interpret them in the light of local circumstances and the needs of young people themselves? And are we quite sure of the rationale for each of these kinds of experiences? Can we legitinately bring extra-curricular activities in from the cold? In this way we might see schooling as only one part of the educational process.

Moving forward

So how can a set of curriculum principles 3–18 actually help? For example, can such principles improve primary–secondary transition? Can they ensure that all pupils receive a fair deal? Can they offer guidance to curriculum planners and managers? Can they enable parents to understand the system better? Will employers have more faith in the system?

But is there also another set of principles which need to be argreed? Are issues such as these important:

- access
- opportunity
- involvement (in decision-making)
- provision?

In other words, is it a right to have access to learning even when the professionals in the system acting (as they see it) in your best interests, conclude that certain experiences or even whole subject areas are not for you? If you do have the opportunity to try something, how will anyone know if you are capable of succeeding? In the mid 1970s the present author, then a principal teacher of English, was asked by a pupil who had been temporarily put, into a 'middle-set' which was to study the play *Spring and Port Wine* while the 'top set' was to study *Romeo and Juliet*, 'Sir, how do you know that I can't do Shakespeare if you don't let me try?' A similar question was put to the same person, by now a headteacher of a comprehensive school by a parent of a pupil who had been assigned to a foundation/general maths set while her best friend (and long time rival in the learning stakes) has been put into the general/credit set. The question, 'Can you assure me that my daughter will have an equal chance to succeed in maths as her friend?', could only be answered in the negative. The truth was that within weeks of starting the course, the two sets would have diverged significantly, the pace of work would have been different and the teachers' expectations would have been different too. Thus access is not simply about physically being there, it is about the belief system which underpins the process of education and whether levels (at 5–14 or Standard Grade) become labels which limit the opportunities for success.

Remembrance of Things Past

Now that we have entered the twenty-first century, the temptation is to look forward to the new challenges which we will all have to face. Yet we cannot do so without looking at the lessons of the past, the successes and the failures. One of these 'failures' was the Report of the Advisory Council on Education in Scotland; Secondary Education, published in 1947. It was a failure insofar as its recommendations were not acted upon. However, its chapter on 'The Aim of the Secondary Education' reminds us of the need to look at the needs of the individual of the society in which s/he lives:

> What is the aim of secondary education is a question that admits of no answer without a reference to ultimate convictions about human nature and destiny, about society and how the individual stands related to it. Merely to change singular to plural and list a variety of desirable aims is no help, for education then becomes an arena of conflicting claims and the question persists – what is the end and what merely means, what has first place and what is subordinate?
>
> (Ch. iv 47)

Three decades later, Education 10–14 in Scotland has phrased it slightly more succinctly, suggesting that schools:

> ...help children to acquire the competences they need to operate effectively and ethically in society, and to help them to understand and make sense of themselves and their world.

The transition from primary to secondary school is a key stage in the educational development of young people. It may require some radical thinking to make the experience continuous, progressive and coherent but we can take some solace from the fact that advice from the past may still help us prepare children for their future.

Endnote: PPP and primary–secondary transition

What is certainly true is that more of the same will not be enough to meet the challenges of primary–secondary transition. It is regrettable that in response to government pressure to reduce surplus places in secondary school, many councils have rushed to construct new buildings which simply take as their starting point the present curriculum structures. Soon these same councils will re-build their primary schools, and for the next 30 to 40 years, the present primary–secondary divide will remain institutionalised. There is still a chance for those councils who have not rushed in the Public Private Partnership approach to try some new configurations of schooling, 3–18, to see how the sectors could begin to see themselves as part of a continuous process of education, rather than separate stages.

SUMMARY

Until the establishment of the ministerial review group in the curriculum 3–18 in 2003, there had been no attempts in Scotland to look at the whole of the curriculum from pre-school to upper secondary since the 1947 Advisory Council reports. The review group looked at the characteristics of the kinds of young people they would wish to emerge after some fifteen years in the school system. It looked at aims, values, purposes and principles and tried to arrive at conclusions which would build a consensus across the various stakeholders. The litmus test may be how the final report of the review group can be used to help policy-makers at national and local levels to address key issues of entitlement, core content, equality of opportunity and personalisation of education. Will its report help schools to produce young people who can be fulfilled, contribute positively to a democratic Scotland and face the challenges of a rapidly changing world?

POINTS FOR REFLECTION

1. In your view, why has Scotland had such a propensity for looking at bits of system? Why has it taken so long for another look at the whole of schooling to be deemed important? Are there vested interests in maintaining the *status quo* or does political or professional expediency tend to dominate?

2. Does Feuerstein's claim that 'chromosomes do not have the last word' have any relevance for the way in which we organise education in Scotland?

3. In your view, what is education for?

4. Can McGuinness's view of thinking skills be a way of introducing coherence and continuity into the school system, P6 and S2?

References

Chapter 1

Boyd, B. (1992) *Letting a hundred flowers blossom...* Unpublished PhD Thesis University of Glasgow

Boyd, B. and Simpson, S. (2000) *A framework for learning and teaching in the first two years of secondary school in Angus Council* Angus Council Education Department

Boyd, B. and Lawson, J. (2003) *Guidance Matters* Glasgow University of Strathclyde

Consultative Council on the Curriculum (1986) *Education 10–14 in Scotland: Report of the Programme Directing Committee* Dundee College of Education

Department for Education and Science (1978) *Special Educational Needs: Report of the Committee of Enquiry into the Education of Handicapped Children and Young People* (The Warnock Report) London HMSO

Hamill, P. and Boyd, B. (2000) *Striving for Inclusion* Glasgow University of Strathclyde

Hamill, P. and Boyd, B. (2001) *Taking the Initiative* Glasgow University of Strathclyde

Hamill, P. and Boyd, B. (2003) *Inclusion: principles into practice* Glasgow University of Strathclyde

Hartley, D. and Roger, A. (1990) *Curriculum and Assesssment: a Policy for the 90s* Professional Issues in Education

Harlen, W. and Malcolm, H. (1997) *Setting and Streaming* Edinburgh SCRE

HM Inspectors of Schools (1988) *Effective Secondary Schools* Edinburgh HMSO

HM Inspectors of Schools (1989) *Effective Primary Schools* Edinburgh HMSO

HM Inspectors of Schools (1996) *Achievement for All* Edinburgh HMSO

HM Inspectors of Schools (1997) *Achieving Success in S1 and S2* Edinburgh HMSO

Paterson, L. (2003) *Scottish Education in the Twentieth Century* Edinburgh University Press

Scottish Education Department (1966) *Primary Education in Scotland (The Primary Memorandum)* Edinburgh HMSO

SED (1977, a) *The Structure of the Curriculum in the Third and Fourth Years of the Scottish Secondary School* (The Munn Report) Edinburgh HMSO

SED (1977, b) *Assessment for All: Report of the Committee to Review Assessment in the Third and Fourth Years of Secondary Education in Scotland* (The Dunning Report) Edinburgh HMSO

SED (1978) *The Education of Children with Learning Difficulties in Primary and Secondary Schools – a progress report* Edinburgh HMSO

SED (1981) *Learning and Teaching in P4 and P7* Edinburgh HMSO

Scottish Office Education and Industry Department (1998) *Improving Achievements in Scottish Schools: A Report to the Secretary of State for Scotland* Edinburgh HMSO

Times Educational Supplement Scotland 14 March 2003

Chapter 2

DfES (2003) *Excellence and Enjoyment* London HMSO

Entwistle, N. (1981) *Styles of Teaching and Learning: An Integrated Outline of Educational Psychology for Students, Teachers and Lecturers* Chichester Wiley

Farquharson, E.A. (1990) 'History, Culture and the Pedagogy of the Primary Memorandum' in *Scottish Educational Review* Vol 22 Number 1 May

Harrison, M.M. and Marker, W.B. (1996) *Teaching the Teachers; The History of Jordanhill College of Education 1828–1993* Edinburgh John Donald Publishers

Highland Council (2000) *Moving On: the emotional well-being of young people in transition from primary to secondary school*

Gallasgtegi, L (2004) *Teaching and Learning Spanish in Primary and Early Secondary Schools in West Central Scotland* Unpublished PhD Thesis Glasgow University of Strathclyde

Hirst, P. (1976) *Knowledge and the Curriculum* London Routledge Keegan Paul

Leslie, M. (2003) *Early Intervention in Literacy: a Study of Implementation in Six Scottish Primary School* Unpublished PhD Thesis University of Edinburgh

Macdonald, A. (1994) 'Themes and Subjects' in Kirk , G. and Glaister, R. *5–14: Scotland's National Curriculum* Edinburgh Scottish Academic Press

Paterson, L. (2003) *Scottish Education in the Twentieth Century* Edinburgh University Press

SCCC (1987) *The Structure and Balance of the Curriculum* Edinburgh HMSO

Scottish Education Department (1966) *The Primary Memorandum*

Suffolk Education Department (1996) *A Report of an Investigation into what happens when Pupils transfer into their Next Schools at the Ages of 9, 11 and 13* Suffolk LEA

Chapter 3

Consultative Council on the Curriculum (1986) *Education 10–14 in Scotland* Dundee

Cumming, M. (1996) 'Far from Elementary: initial training for the primary sector' in *Teaching the Teachers* Margaret M, Harrison and Willis B. Marker (Eds) Edinburgh John Donald Publishing

Gatherer, W. (1989) 'Curriculum Development in Scotland' in *Professional Issues in Education* Edinburgh Scottish Academic Press

Kirk, G. (1996) 'The Training of Secondary Teachers' in *Teaching the Teachers* Margaret M, Harrison and Willis B. Marker (Eds) Edinburgh John Donald Publishing

McPherson, A and Raab, C.D. (1988) *Governing Education: A Sociology of Policy since 1945* Edinburgh University Press

Roger, A. and Hartley, D. (1990) *Curriculum and Assessment in Scotland: A Policy for the 90s* Edinburgh Scottish Academic Press

Scottish Education Department (1947) *Secondary Education* Report of the Advisory Council Edinburgh HMSO

Scottish Executive Education Department (2001) *A Teaching Profession for the 21st Century* Edinburgh HMSO

Scottish Office Education Department (1993) *The Education of Able Pupils P6 to S2* Edinburgh HMSO

Scottish Office Education Department; *Curriculum and Assessment: a Policy for the '90s* Edinburgh

Times Educational Supplement Scotland (5 December 2003) 'Special Branch'

Chapter 4

Buzan, T. (1993) *The Mind Map Book: Radiant Thinking* London BBC Books

Buzan, T. (2001) *Head Strong: How to Get Physically and Mentally Fit* London Thorsons

Department of Education and Science (1967) *Children and their Primary Schools* A Report of the Central Advisory Council for Education (The Plowden Report) London HMSO

Feuerstein, R. (1990) 'The theory of structural cognitive modifiability' in Presseisen, B (Ed) *Learning and Thinking Styles: Classroom Interaction* Washington DC National Education Association

Gardner, H. (1993) *Multiple Intelligences: The Theory in Practice* London Harper Collins

Gatherer, W. (1989) *Curriculum Development in Scotland* Professional Issues in Education Edinburgh Scottish Academic Press

Getzels, J. W. and Jackson, P. W. (1962) *Creativity and Intelligence* New York Wiley

Goleman, D. (1996) *Emotional Intelligence* London Bloomsbury

Hannaford, C. (1995) *Smart Moves: Why Learning is Not All Inside Your Head* Hawaii Jamilla Nur Publishing

Herrnstein, R.J. and Murray, C. (1994) *The Bell Curve: Intelligence and class structure in American life* New York Free Press

Jensen, A. (1969) 'How much can we boost intelligence and scholastic achievement?' *Harvard Educational Review* 39(1) 1–123

Jensen, E. (1994) *The Learning Brain* San Diego Turning Point Publishing

Kogan, N. and Wallach, M.A. (1964) *Risk-Taking: A Study in Cognition and Personality* New York Rinehart and Winston

Levy, J. (1988) 'Research Synthesis on Right and Left Hemispheres: We Think with Both Sides of the Brain' *Educational Leadership* 40.4: 66–71

Lipman, M. (2003) *Thinking in Education* Cambridge University Press

Mosley, J (1995) *Turn Your School Around* Cambridge IDA

Piaget,J. (1976) *The Grasp of Consciousness: Action and Concept in the Young Mind* Cambridge MA Harvard University Press

Scottish Education Department (1965) *The Primary Memorandum* Edinburgh HMSO

Smith, I. (2000) *How does the brain learn?* Occasional Paper 1 Glasgow Learning Unlimited

Sperry, R. (1968) 'Hemisphere Disconnection and Unity in Conscious Awareness' *American Psychologist* 23: 723–733

The Department for Education and Skills (2003) *Education and Excellence* London DfES Publications

Vygotsky, L.S. (1986) *Thought and Language* Ed. Alex Kozulin Cambridge MA MIT Press

Chapter 5

Bantock, G.H. (1980) *Dilemmas of the Curriculum* London Martin Robertson

Barber, Michael (1994) *Young People and their Attitudes to School* Keele Keele University

Cox, C.B. and Boyson, R. (1969) *Fight for education: a Black Paper* London Critical Quarterly Society

Her Majesty's Inspectorate of Education (2000) *Educating the Whole Child* Edinburgh HMSO

Scottish Executive Education Department (2003) *Educating for Excellence*

Strathclyde Regional Council (1992) *Every Child is Special*

Chapter 6

Black, P and Wiliam, D. (1998) *Inside the Black Box: Raising standards through classroom assessment* London School of Education King's College

Boyd, B. (1994) *Of Drunks and Lampposts* Glasgow University of Strathclyde

Boyd, B. (2004) 'To set or not to set: is that the question?' in *Improving Schools* (Forthcoming) Stoke-on-Trent Trentham Books

DfES (2003) *Educating for Excellence* London DfES Publications

Harlen,W and Malcolm, H. (1997) *Setting and Streaming: a Research Review* Edinburgh SCRE

Smith, C., M. M. and Sutherland, M., J. (2002) *Setting or mixed ability? Pupils' views of the organisational arrangements in their school* Paper presented at the Scottish Educational Research Association Conference, Dundee September 2002

Smith, C. M. M. and Sutherland, M., J. (2003) 'Setting or mixed ability? Teachers' views of the organisation of pupils for learning' in *Journal of Research in Special Educational Needs* V3, N3, pp141–6

SOEID (1996) *Achievement for All* Edinburgh HMS0

SOED (1993) *The Education of Able Pupils P6 to S2* Edinburgh HMSO

Chapter 7

Boyd, B. and Lawson, J. (2003) *Guidance Matters* Glasgow University of Strathclyde

Delamont, S. and Galton, M. (1986) *Inside the Secondary Classroom* London Routledge and Kegan Paul

Feuerstein, R. (1990) 'The theory of structural cognitive modifiability' in *Learning and Thinking Styles: Classroom Interaction* Presseisen, B (Ed) Washington DC National Education Association

McLean, A. (2003) *The Motivated School* London Paul Chapman Publishing

Rudduck, J, Chaplain, R. and Wallace, G. (Eds) (1996) *School Improvement: What can pupils tell us?* London David Fulton Publishers

Silberman, M.L. (1971) 'Discussion' in *The Experience of Schooling* M.L. Silberman (Ed) New York Holt, Rinehart and Winston

SNAP@educ.gla.ac.uk

SOEID (1996) *Achievement for All* Edinburgh HMSO

SOEID (1997) *Achieving Success in S1 and S2* Edinburgh HMSO

Chapter 8

Boyd, B. and Simpson, S. (2000) *A framework for learning and teaching in the first two years of secondary school in Angus Council* Angus Council Education Department

Galton, M., Gray, J. and Rudduck, J. (2003) *FfEE Research Brief No, 131 The Impact of Transitions and Transfers on Pupil Progress* University of Cambridge Homerton College

Times Education Supplement Scotland, 5 December 2003

Chapter 9

Appleton (2003) *Review of Curricular Approaches in Other Countries* Scottish Executive Education Department

Core Curriculum for Primary, Secondary and Adult Education in Norway (2002)

Scottish Education Department (1947) *Report of the Advisory Council on Education*

Chapter 10

Buzan, T. (2001) *Head Strong: How to Get Physically and Mentally Fit* London Thorsons

Feuerstein, R. (1990) 'The theory of structural cognitive modifiability' in *Learning and Thinking Styles: Classroom Interaction* B. Pressen (Ed.), Washington, DC National Education Association

Gardner H. (1993) *Multiple Intelligences: The Theory in Practice* London Harper Collins

Goleman, D. (1996) *Emotional Intelligence* London Bloomsbury

Hannaford, C. (1995) *Smart Moves: Why Learning is Not All Inside Your Head* Hawaii Jamilla Nur Publishing

Kirkwood, M. (2005) *Learning to Think: Thinking to Learn* Paisley Hodder Gibson

Kolb, D. A. (1977) *Learning Style Inventory: A Self-description of Preferred learning Modes* Boston, MA McBer

Scottish Executive Education Department (2004) *Assessment is for Learning: Development Programme Interim Report* Dundee Learning and Teaching Scotland

Scottish Office Education Department (1987) *Curriculum and Assessment: a Policy for the 90s*

Sperry, R. (1968) 'Hemisphere Disconnection and Unity in Conscious Awareness' *American Psychologist* 23: 723–733

Further Reading

Boyd, B. and Simpson, M. (2003) *Primary–Secondary Liaison in Scottish Education: Second Edition Post-Devolution* Edinburgh University Press pp 362 – 368

Bryce, T.G.K. and Humes, W.M. (2003) *Scottish Education: Second Edition Post-Devolution* Edinburgh University Press

Fisher, R. (1990) *Teaching Children to Think* Cheltenham Neslon Thornes

Gow, L. and McPherson, A. (1980) *Tell them from me* Aberdeen University Press

Harlen, W. and Malcolm, H. (1997) *Setting and Streaming* Edinburgh Scottish Council for Research in Education

Ireson, J. and Hallam, S. (2001) *Ability Grouping in Education* London Paul Chapman Publishing

Lipman, M.(2003) *Thinking in Education* Cambridge University Press

Millard, E. (1997) *Differently Literate: Boys, Girls and the Schooling of Literacy* London Falmer Press

Mobilia, W and Gordon, R. (1998) *Education by Design: The Critical Skills Program* New Hampshire Antioch New England Graduate School rgordon@antiochne.edu

Index